Why kill yourself?

Why kill yourself?

MY HEART ATTACK
AND HOW TO PREVENT YOURS

Bernard Falk
& Dr Roger Blackwood

LONDON
VICTOR GOLLANCZ LTD
1987

First published in Great Britain 1987
by Victor Gollancz Ltd,
14 Henrietta Street, London WC2E 8QJ

British Library Cataloguing in Publication Data
Falk, Bernard
    Why kill yourself?: my heart attack
    and how to prevent yours.
    1. Coronary heart diseases—Prevention
    I. Title   II. Blackwood, Roger
    616.1'2305   RC685.C6

ISBN 0-575-04006-8

Photoset in Great Britain by
Rowland Phototypesetting Ltd, Bury St Edmunds, Suffolk
and printed by Billings & Son Ltd, Worcester

Dedicated to Tony
with our prayers that he makes it

Acknowledgements

The authors would like to thank a variety of people for their help and support. First, one another for putting up with the sheer hell of writing it, but in grovelling gratitude to those who made the book possible. Our thanks to Bernard's heart which is the villain of the piece but our heartiest congratulations that, at the moment, it is still ticking.

Roger Blackwood thanks Melissa Ludbrook for typing the impossibly long and complicated medical words so well and Bernard Falk is hoping that Maggie Charlebois and Louise Rawlings who checked and typed his manuscripts will learn to forgive and forget and speak to him again.

Collectively we thank, in total admiration, the doctors and staff at the Nuffield Hospital, Slough, and the National Heart Hospital in London, with particular gratitude to Dr Kim Fox. Also our thanks to all those who work so magnificently for the Slough Health Habit, the East Berkshire Health Authority and Angela Cristofoli, the Community Care dietician at King Edward VII Hospital, Windsor, and the Dietetic Promotion Unit.

Al Murray, former British Olympic weightlifting champion who runs the City Gym in New Union Street, London, gave up his valuable time to instruct Bernard on the dangers of stress. Al and his superb staff of expert instructors are admired by doctors for their work in coping with 2,000 cardiac patients over the years. Poor souls. They have the job of getting Bernard fit and healthy again with a series of exercise programmes geared to pulse rate and careful medical monitoring.

We also wish to thank Jill Ballin, a hard-working producer with the BBC's 'Breakfast Time' programme for her excellent support in producing a series of films echoing the theme of this book, and Carlo Roberto for his brutally honest but very funny cartoons.

The miracle is that everyone associated with the project has not suffered a heart attack themselves but Bernard wishes to make it known that if Roger Blackwood is around they are in safe hands.

B.F. and R.B.
November 1986

Contents

1 Introduction   *page* 11

2 What a lovely bonny baby   20

3 Young at heart   36

4 On the road   52

5 Suicide is painless   75

6 The home straight   83

7 The big day   98

8 A broken heart   109

9 The wounded warrior   126

10 The outpatient and back to work   148

11 Chips with everything   161

12 For the technical or those who can pronounce
    the names   168

13 The patient and the doctor   170

14 How will heart disease be treated in the
    future?   181

15 Conclusion   185

    Appendix: The Slough Health Habit   189

1. Introduction

BERNARD FALK

I cannot remember exactly where I was when it began, an event of such profound importance to me that it would dominate the rest of my life.

But I remember the pain. It grew upon me gradually, increasing in various levels of intensity during two weeks of a sunny spring in 1986. At first I was conscious of a dull ache lying deep within the inside cavity of my chest. It spread into the shoulder along the left arm, a throbbing pain ebbing and flowing like a muscular spasm until it reached my fingers which tingled along the tips. It always arrived first thing in the morning a few minutes after struggling out of bed. It lasted about five or six minutes and reached a climax which took my breath away.

Of course I've always been a clever dick, someone who laughed at the possibility that the way I was living could place my health at risk. 'It can't be,' you think. 'It can't be happening to me. I'm not ill.'

'Overweight, a bit breathless climbing up the stairs, exhausted in the evenings after slogging away at work. But not me. I might smoke twenty cigars a day, perhaps I do drink too much and work too hard under pressure. But I'm young. I feel well. Sickness is for other people. Not me. I don't get killed in car crashes. Aeroplanes do not drop out of the sky when I'm on them. Buildings do not collapse around me. I am never killed by fires, earthquakes, floods, famine or drought. IT WILL NEVER HAPPEN TO ME.'

Such is the insensitivity of those who have always enjoyed boisterous good health that illness seems like a dirty thing, unclean, to be ignored. Someone bent on personal destruction can act with a quite numbing stupidity too.

So there I was with a pain, arriving about three times a day

often after meals and strangely never during the limited amount
of exercise I took, and neither did it come during stressful
periods in a busy working life. I saw doctors, several of them,
and they put it down to a digestive problem, indigestion rather
than a problem with my heart. It is no consolation to realise
that doctors can be stupid too. And yet the body was intelligent
enough to offer its own warning that after so many years of
gambling with my health, my luck was running out. Couldn't
we realise that the evidence screamed: 'BERNARD FALK, YOU
IDIOT, IT'S YOUR HEART. YOU ARE KILLING YOURSELF.' No one,
the doctors, my family, friends, colleagues at work and least
of all myself took the slightest bit of notice. My body had cried
in vain.

Doctors call it a myocardial infarction: a blood clot which
blocks an artery of the heart. It's a heart attack to you and me
and it hurts like hell. After two weeks of regular short attacks
the ache became an agony, an agony of such searing intensity
that it made me want to scream. The dull throb had changed
to a pain which ripped through the left side of my body forcing
me to gasp for breath. It happened at my office in London and
I hid in the toilet to avoid my colleagues seeing a grown man
with tears of pain running down his cheeks. I drove home
through the rush hour traffic on a Friday evening. The pain
went on and on. At home I was examined by a doctor, and a
cardiologist called Dr Roger Blackwood arrived in my life. At
the time how could I have realised that he would not only help
to save my life but later have a permanent influence upon the
way I would have to change it. Then, in my bedroom, I saw
him through a blur of pain, a tall beanpole of a man strapping
a strange-looking contraption to my chest. It was a portable
electro-cardiograph machine – an ECG – which Roger carries
around in a briefcase. I remember him gently suggesting that
maybe I should be in hospital. 'Just to sort out what's wrong
old chap,' he said. An hour later I was in intensive care. The
following morning the pain had gone and the heart attack was
over.

Later they told me I was lucky. How lucky I only began to
realise during six weeks of rest, rehabilitation and a realisation
that if my life was to continue there would have to be radical
changes in the way I chose to live it.

I was 43 with a pregnant wife, four other children, a relatively successful career and at the threshold of financial success running my own video production company. 1986 was a year to remember, but not because I had a heart attack which could have killed me, but because I survived one. Furthermore I have lived to realise that from childhood to the present day my way of life had been designed to place my health at risk.

I am sure everyone has said at one time, 'If only I could start again,' to forget, to cancel what has gone before. A heart attack brings you down to earth. What must be done to avoid being buried beneath it long before your time? For so many years I deliberately walked a tightrope between a reasonably healthy life and total neglect. I've always known that the body is a machine that needs care and servicing but I never bothered to take the machine to a garage or consult an expert mechanic. It was a source of pride that for ten years I never saw a doctor or took a day off work due to illness. Now those years of neglect seem like a tragic waste. I am wounded, physically in a small region around the heart, but psychologically too. To be honest I feel a fool. And, in solitary moments when I think about what went wrong inside, I am more than a little frightened too.

I emerged from intensive care with grateful thanks to the kind, skilled and dedicated medical and nursing staff of the Nuffield Hospital in Slough with time to consider what I should do to change the habits of a lifetime. Dieting? I adore good food. Healthy eating then? My favourite meal is a mixed grill with lots of chips. Reduce pressure and stress? I never realised I suffered from either. Spend less time working? I love work and feel deprived without it. Give up smoking? Pure hell when you're addicted to forty cigarettes a day. It is not easy to change habits of a lifetime and yet none of it matters a hoot unless we learn to understand that it is human behaviour which leads us into trouble.

More than anything I have learned that heart attacks are not inevitable. God or the evolutionary process did not decide that one specific organ of the body, an organ of such importance that its complete failure brings instant death, should be weaker than any other. The heart is a pump, more complex in design and structure than many other vital organs but no weaker or stronger than a liver, a brain, an armpit, a backbone or your little toe. So there must be a reason why heart failure kills more people than any other human disease.

I now realise that my heart attack was a warning from a body collapsing under the sheer weight of its proprietor's own stupidity. Of course some people have weak or damaged hearts, often at birth, and this is a physical malfunction which cannot be blamed on lifestyle. But most cases of heart disease in our fast-moving technological society are caused by human ignorance, neglect, indifference and quite mind-boggling arrogance. Government, health services, the medical profession and all the rest of us are responsible for this mass extermination of our own species. Right now millions of others have already embarked on the journey towards a premature death. We are killing ourselves even though this ghastly self-inflicted human tragedy could be avoided if only we have the will.

The biggest enemy is our own apathy to the problem and our ignorance of what is purely a disease of the latter part of the twentieth century. So before tackling the epidemic we need to know much more about the history of heart attacks which means tracing the killer to its source.

DR ROGER BLACKWOOD. CARDIOLOGIST

For hundreds of years it was thought that the heart was immune to disease. For when Joan of Arc was burnt at the stake in 1431 her heart remained quite unaffected after the rest of her was burnt to ashes and, despite covering it in oil and throwing it back on the fire, it refused to burn. And so symptoms such as pain in the chest were thought to have nothing to do with the heart. It is remarkable that, over five hundred years later, such symptoms are still ignored.

Angina, caused by the narrowing of the blood vessels of the heart, is a condition which is extremely common today. Yet when it was first described in 1768 no mention was made of the heart as the source of the problem. Gradually, as more post-mortems were performed it was realised that the heart could be abnormal and a potent source of symptoms. But 'heart attacks' were not identified until about 1870 and then only after the patient had died. Hammer, an American, and

Sir Richard Quain wrote the first descriptions of what is now known as a heart attack although it was referred to then as 'fatty degeneration'.

Heart attacks were rare at that time and the greatest professor of the day, Sir William Osler, Regius Professor of Medicine at Oxford, wrote that junior doctors would never actually *see* an attack and consultants might diagnose it after death only about half a dozen times a year. It was not until in 1912 that a patient was shown to have survived a heart attack, albeit it for a very short time. By the 1920s, more and more heart attacks were being diagnosed, at first by symptoms and signs but later by an electro-cardiograph machine (an ECG machine) which became the cardiologist's standard tool.

This machine, invented by Einthoven, records the electrical signals produced by the heart. The first ever electrical signals had been recorded from a tortoise in 1875 directly from the surface of the heart – which is clearly impractical in a human patient. With Einthoven's machine the patient had to stand with each leg in a bucket of water and one arm in a third. Fortunately since then technology has moved on so that when I went to Bernard's home the recording of the electrical activity of his heart was extremely simple.

Only in the 1940s did it dawn that the incidence of heart attacks was rising at a phenomenal rate. The official figure in 1910 had been 939 heart attacks in the whole year in the whole of Great Britain. By 1954, it was 65,671 and now in the mid 1980s it is well over 200,000 a year. Many people thought that perhaps doctors had just misdiagnosed the condition in the nineteenth century or had called it by some other name. However by the 1940s post-mortems had begun to show narrowed arteries of the heart very frequently indeed, whereas during the last century this had been very much the exception.

The late 1940s saw the birth of the National Health Service which, it was thought, would cost less and less as infection, the major cause of illness then, would be controlled. However, no one had bargained on the rise of heart attacks which, by the 1950s, had reached epidemic proportions. Up and up went the figures until by the 1970s it was the biggest single cause of death, and remains so today.

When I first examined Bernard it was easy for me as a

cardiologist to identify that his severe chest pains were due to a heart attack. This showed up on my portable ECG machine. In simple terms a heart attack is the abrupt blockage of an artery of the heart.

It is also called a 'coronary' or in technical terms 'a myocardial infarction'. The abrupt blockage tends to happen at an already narrow part of the coronary artery. The narrowing, rather like the furring-up of water pipes, is caused by a fatty material or cholesterol being laid down on the inside of the arteries. Many of us will begin to develop these narrowings of the arteries of the heart as a teenager. During the Korean War it was discovered that an astonishingly high proportion of young American soldiers, on whom post-mortems were carried out—about 50 per cent—were already showing signs of this narrowing process. This was not the case with the Korean and Chinese soldiers who showed none at all.

The process of narrowing is extremely slow but eventually it will either completely block the artery, in other words you will have a heart attack, or there will be so much narrowing that any exertion you make may bring on pain. This is angina. The British Heart Foundation tells us that 44 per cent of all deaths under the age of 65 are caused by artery problems. This reveals the enormity of the problem.

If you were to compare the death rate from heart attacks, country by country, you will see that some countries such as Japan have always had a much lower incidence of heart attacks than the United Kingdom, but the United States, which started with almost the same incidence as ours, has shown more than a 25 per cent drop.

Why this has happened is because of a change in the risk factors involved. In the United States a sensible diet, jogging and a dramatic fall in smoking, coupled with an improvement in general health care such as reducing high blood pressure, has become part of the way of life for many people.

In other words, if people eat less fat, smoke less and generally take better care of themselves, they are less likely to have heart attacks. However one must be wary of statistics: in the 1950s and 1960s the incidence of heart attacks was exactly the same as the increase in the number of television licences. Obviously we cannot blame television for heart attacks (or else people like Bernard would have a lot to answer for) and we shall be dealing with the real risk factors later. What can be argued is that improvements in general medicine and better technology could lead to an earlier detection of disease, and hence to better prevention by tablets, for example, rather than by improved lifestyle. But even taking this possibility into account it cannot explain the dramatic fall in the United States. In contrast the death rate in Britain remains alarmingly high because our attitudes to health are apathetic.

Men are more likely to have heart attacks than women—until women reach the age of the menopause. This is probably due to female hormones. But women catch up with men remarkably quickly afterwards.

In the United States in the last fifteen years there has been a 30 per cent reduction in the death rate in women with heart attacks, more even than in men. In Britain the figures have remained depressingly constant. More women in the United Kingdom smoke than ever before and an alarming 45 per cent of sixteen-year-old girls appear to smoke fairly regularly. In one study of women the average age of death for heavy smokers was an extraordinary nineteen years earlier than non-smokers.

Why has Britain fallen so far behind? Where have we gone wrong? And what can we do to reduce our quite appalling death rate due to heart disease? Our major problem is one of attitude. Bernard himself admits that he never took health care seriously and so many others believe that they can ignore a sensible lifestyle.

In this country preventive medicine is seen as boring and goody-goody. There is still a macho image associated with cigarette smoking. What is more, doctors have little incentive to practise preventive medicine. There is no provision under the National Health Service for a patient who goes to his GP merely wanting a check-up. He may have to pay over £150 for a private medical to achieve what he wants and this cost is prohibitive to most people. The GP simply does not have the time to spend forty minutes on one patient, taking a history, examining him, organising a chest X-ray, electro-cardiogram and blood test. Don't forget that the GP already has surgeries bulging with patients and has to allow about five to eight minutes for each one.

Nor is practising preventive medicine quite how the doctor sees his role in life. If he is called to a cardiac arrest and heroically saves a patient's life, he has an overwhelming feeling of satisfaction. Compare that with telling a patient to stop smoking. He may save the patient's life but he will never know for certain and in the process of telling him not to smoke the patient may get very irritated with him, which does neither the patient nor the doctor any good at all.

If these reasons are true, why is it that in the United States people are bothering about their health? Ironically it is probably due to the National Health Service itself. In the States it is so expensive to be ill for any length of time because of the enormous medical bills. So people actually try to avoid becoming ill in the first place. In Britain there is a feeling that 'they'—the NHS—will take care of you in every way including financially. Thus preventive medicine is less prominent in this country.

In all honesty, despite millions of pounds spent on research we do not know precisely why someone has a heart attack. What we do know are the risk factors which make one person more likely to have a heart attack in comparison with another.

But in Britain tradition plays a prominent role in pretty well everything including the way we live and health consiousness is changing only slowly. School meals have changed very little over the years, and more and more schoolgirls smoke than ever before.

The Government has put a lot of money into television advertising in particular about the dangers of smoking with little apparent effect. Perhaps this is because a health advert on television never really applies to you personally but always to some other people whoever they might be. This is why a more personalised programme such as the Slough Health Habit has been developed and why it is so successful (see Appendix on p. 189).

The constant feedback that I receive when talking about heart attacks is that: 'We all have to die of something. It might as well be a heart attack. After all, death is sudden at that.' But heart attacks affect large numbers of people in the prime of life rather than in advanced old age. For those who are left behind this is an emotional and financial disaster, never mind a waste of so many valuable years of life for the victims.

In 1981 the cost of heart attacks in the United States was estimated to be $50,000,000,000. But think of that statistic in human terms and you can understand the scale of the problem.

2. What a lovely bonny baby

BERNARD FALK

I was brought up in Liverpool just after the Second World War. You could tell there had been a war. Huge chunks of the unfortunate place were missing, knocked flat by a mysterious race of people my father described as 'Jerry bastards'. I quickly related this to a structure called an air-raid shelter in our back garden.

Sam Falk ran a wines and spirits business which he and his twin brother Joe inherited from their stern Victorian father. By rights it should have been called Sam and Joe Falk of Liverpool. But they came from imaginative East European Jewish stock, so our company revelled in names stolen from the local telephone directory—Barker, Rogers, Soughall Co. Ltd, of Liverpool, Glasgow, London, Paris and Rome. It was a cellar with two rooms tucked under a grubby street just off Liverpool docks. This is how self-delusion begins.

Compared with most of my fellow citizens growing up in a battered city which had suffered six years of war we were relatively well off. Home was a detached three-bedroomed house with a garden. The other houses in the road were semis which made my mother, Linda, feel like a duchess. And we were in the suburbs.

My parents had put down a deposit of £2 10s. to have their home built soon after they were married. This elevated us to a life among the middle class and when I was born in 1943 we were far enough away from the scruffs who lived in the city itself. Life for a little boy, for a spoiled only child, was good: comfortable, loving, secure. It never occurred to people of my parents' generation that the way we led our lives could cause serious health problems in the future. It is desperately unfair to an adoring mother and father, but my generation began killing itself forty years ago. Sadly our parents, or the

And life for a little boy, for a spoiled only
child, was good . . .

society of the time, must bear much of the responsibility, and when it comes to health care most of us remain just as irresponsible, or ignorant today.

Sam was always on the tubby side or at least he was when we first got acquainted and he was already in his forties. A faded picture on my mother's dressing-table shows a very different man: thin and fit with curly black hair, a reminder that he and his brother Joe lied about their ages and enlisted in the British Army when they were sixteen to fight in Palestine during the Great War.

My mother loved Sam. She still does even though he's been dead for nearly thirty years. But such is the somewhat unique humour of Liverpudlians that love can be totally suppressed by abuse. 'You look like a pregnant duck,' said Mum in an observation of Sam walking. 'With constipation,' as an afterthought.

And to be fair he did waddle along. His big tum would move up and down on top of two spindly legs as he attempted the elementary business of placing one leg in front of the other, on the exceedingly rare occasions when he condescended to walk. To cope with this seemingly impossible task Sam discovered the perfect compromise. He sat. Others walked, which seemed fair enough until you reflect forty years later what this might have done to his health.

Sam wasn't very fat nor to my recollection did he have a big appetite. It's just that everything seemed to be in the wrong place and like 99 per cent of other families we knew nothing about the importance of a carefully balanced diet or healthy eating. Furthermore Sam really hated exercise. His idea of a perfect day out was to get in his smart car and drive Mother and me off for a day out in Southport. There we would have a slap-up meal in a restaurant and then all of us would sit on a park bench and watch other people walking by. It never entered Sam's head to join them in this activity. Likewise when we had the special treat of going to the Southport fun fair with its big dipper, dodgems and roundabouts, I joined in the frantic activities on my own. Dad was happy to sit and watch. Then off home with some lovely greasy fish and chips on the way, eaten from real newspapers and served with lashings of salt and vinegar. After a slumber by the fire

watching our newly acquired twelve-inch television set it was
off to bed at the end of a perfect day. Or was it?

You wonder so many years later what Sam's attitude to
health and exercise did to my perception of the way I should
lead my life? Dad didn't play. He sat. His idea of having fun
was to watch other people having fun. He never played soccer,
cricket, or swam, certainly in my memory of him. It is hard
to level blame at a man who adored his only child. But did I
start killing myself then—sitting alongside Dad watching other
fathers kick a football with their kids? Certainly I've never
found it easy to play with my own children even though I love
them just as much as he loved me. And play is the earliest
form of exercise. I am 43, the same age as Sam when he became
a father for the one and only time, and I can see now that we
have very similar attitudes.

Like Sam I have always placed effort under the category of
success in business or career. We were both proud of our
families but also what our efforts could give them in material
comforts rather than pure companionship. My own children
accuse me today of not spending enough time with them. I
have always been too busy, building up a career in journalism
and later business and likewise Sam's life was dominated by
business, acquiring possessions, guaranteeing financial security, buying my mother nice clothes and me lots of toys.
He was a family man and as companions my parents were
inseparable. He never went out on his own for a drink, we
always took holidays together. But ask him to play cricket, go
for a walk, do some keep-fit exercises, swim in the sea, climb
a hill, even touch his toes and a look of panic would cross his
face.

Sam did not move much. He was an excellent businessman,
kind and generous. But when I wanted to learn to sail a small
boat he was delighted to buy it and pay for someone else to
teach me. It never entered Sam's head to learn how to sail it
himself. How much of this was due to a wide age gap between
himself and me I cannot tell. But I used to envy other children
their more vibrant, active fathers whooping it up on the beach
or running in a field. Sam watched. Others did, except when
it came to running his business or swamping his family with
love.

Mother was an entirely different kettle of fish and still is, living and caring for herself in her own home, driving her car, at the age of 83. Interesting that she has never smoked or drunk alcohol and has hardly ever been overweight. Nowadays she has a slight muscular problem but otherwise is fighting fit, mentally agile, a tough wiry old bird whom we expect to outlive all of us. In fact unless I make radical changes to my lifestyle she could easily outlive her only son. Like my father she came from a big family and was the second youngest. And if there's one rule under which she has always led her life then it was to ensure that once married her family always got the best of everything. This meant a considerable amount of social climbing for Mum born to a decent working-class family and an enormous amount of encouragement to Sam as he struggled to build up a small business.

It was Mum who pushed Sam into buying their own home, Mum who persuaded him to pay for me to be educated privately at local prep and public schools, and I believe she was the major influence on the size of her family. There was to be one only. Me. I was going to be the sole recipient of my parents' love. In other words I was spoiled rotten and loved every minute of it. But you wonder how much damage that caused? What I wanted I normally got, whether or not it was good for me and that has tended to be a driving force throughout my life. Call it ambition if you like but others might say I have always been selfish and self-indulgent.

To understand what influence this may have played in the problems I have experienced with my heart forty-odd years later it is necessary to transport ourselves into the type of society in which we lived during the early years of post-war Britain. Rationing was still in force and it dominated the way our families ate and catered for themselves. During the war life seemed to revolve around what you were allowed and what you could get on the 'nudge-nudge' principle from the local butcher. 'He slipped me an extra sausage under the counter,' my mother would say proudly. Then there was the black market. My father ran a wines and spirits business throughout the war and one wonders what extra little goodies came our way in exchange for the odd bottle of Scotch. Certainly I can never remember us being deprived of anything except for the near-impossible, like real eggs, cream, fresh tropical fruit, chocolates, or all the things our kids take for granted now. The society in which I was brought up seemed dedicated to extracting that little bit extra out of the system. My parents, more capable than most in catering for their own, joined in the rat-race with considerable enthusiasm and no small measure of success. I had a toy train before the other kids. We had steak when the others had faggots. We were the first in the street with a television set. Our garden was bigger than the others in the street and it was the only one with a swing. I know it sounds enormously selfish and perhaps it was but it is no more than I have attempted to achieve for my own family. It is only later when you begin to think of the consequences that you can think back on those days with a measure of regret.

My mother's generation was brought up on the 'bouncing bonny baby' concept. Healthy babies were chubby. They weren't fat. Just bonny. And Mum was determined that her beautiful little boy was going to be chubbier and bonnier than any other little fink in the street. The guiding principle of parenthood in my mother's generation was: 'Fill 'em up. Bung 'em up with grub and they'll grow up healthy and strong.' In those days it would be unthinkable to suggest that taking large quantities of milk, sugar, or red meat might be unhealthy. If you could get the stuff then in it went and the more the merrier. Fresh vegetables were hard to obtain and apart from apples and pears grown locally fresh fruit was unavailable. There were occasional concessions to commonsense. 'An apple a day keeps the doctor away' was an early expression I remember. But generally mothers fried food rather than grilled it. Chips with everything was the norm. Indeed if you compare today's trend towards healthier eating we lived in the Third World when I was a boy.

With rationing, the deprivation experienced by parents who had lived through two world wars plus the insecure and frightening hungry Thirties, is it any wonder that a fashion for unhealthy eating was ingrained in our lifestyle? If you could get food you ate it. Children were encouraged or bribed to eat everything on their plates and were often threatened with punishment if they refused. Indeed parents make the same mistake today. Never mind that little Jimmy is so bunged up

with food he cannot move. Eating everything up guarantees
he'll grow up to be healthy and strong. What nonsense. If a
child doesn't want to eat, it is because he's either not hungry
or ill. Or maybe the portions are too big.

My mother's very specialist brand of torture was to make a
hideous concoction called a rice pudding. This revolting glue-
like substance was placed before me as though it was a glorious
culinary achievement. It was probably very nutritious, providing you ate nothing else for a week. Any sign of refusal—like
throwing up—was met with the words, 'The starving children
of Asia would just love this rice pudding.' I only prayed she
would sent it to them; and my mother, being a very determined
lady, would serve up the same rice pudding for every meal
until I eventually ate it. It never occurred to our parents to
question what our eating habits were doing to our health, and
school only compounded what was to become the national
tragedy of a heart disease epidemic in the years to come.

Liverpool College is one of Britain's minor public schools
and it educates the prosperous middle class of the city. It lies
in Sefton Park, a beautiful oasis of greenery in the middle of
one of Britain's least attractive urban environments. By the
time I arrived, bunged up with too much rice pudding, I was
already overweight, a little tubby Jewish kid looking like a
junior version of his Dad. From the start I began to suspect
that the other kids didn't like me. This was not particularly
perceptive. The highlight of any break was chucking Falk on
to the concrete floor of the playground and jumping up and
down on his head. This was usually accompanied by some
advice like, 'Drop dead you dirty Yid'. Of course it was a
Protestant school but they weren't necessarily anti-Semitic.
They just hated Jews. The masters, who wore gallantry medals
for bashing the Hun in the war, joined in the general fun. In
the space of a few weeks I was beaten on the bum with a
cane, the foot-rest of a desk, a running pump, a copy of the
Encyclopedia Britannica (A–D edition) and a wooden spoon.

Perhaps they were trying to reduce my bum in size by
battering it to death—a kind of primitive version of Slender-
tone. Maybe they just disliked Jews, but more likely they
disliked me for being a stroppy, arrogant little sod with an
exaggerated sense of my own importance. Anyway I hated

We were the first in the street with a
television set . . .

school and it hated me. The only thing I learned was how to play poker, with the other Jewish kids while the rest of the school prayed in Chapel.

Another outstanding achievement was managing to unclip a suspender from the *inside* worn by a pretty maid in the school canteen as she served up even more rice pudding for lunch. I got flogged for that as well.

Which brings me to school meals. Oh! what priceless memories they conjure up. To think that there are generations of ex-public school chaps in faded old boys' blazers sitting on the verandah of some sweaty foreign field, drinking their Sundowners and dreaming with nostalgia of matron's knickers and prep school dinners. The pungent smell of lumpy spuds, spam fritters, overcooked cabbage, spotted dick, treacle pie, bread-and-butter pud, roly-poly sponge, corned beef and chips: it's enough to make a modern-day dietician weep. And the situation is not much better now. What on earth have we done to the eating habits of our young? The people who devised the meals at my school knew nothing about nutrition. Like at home, meals were designed to satisfy hungry young appetites, to fill up huge aching spaces in the belly and the more stodge the better.

The little fat Jewish kid grew bigger and turned into a big fat Jewish kid with an appetite like a horse, a deep hatred for vegetables, fruit, fish, or anything remotely healthy. When I emerged from school to enter the world outside I was 16, overweight and determined on a life devoid of exercise. So the rot had begun already and would progress through adolescence into manhood. What a pity I did not heed the danger signs. Indeed the clearest warning of all was a very personal domestic tragedy from which my mother has never recovered.

For the last two years of his life Sam had complained of pains in his chest. They came during the very limited amount of exercise he took. A short walk up the street to post a letter would make him gasp with pain and he was constantly short of breath. For most of his adult life Sam, like so many others of his generation, was a very heavy smoker, getting through about sixty untipped heavy-tar cigarettes a day. Then it was normal. Most people smoked. It was unfashionable not to. Apart from that he was about two stone overweight and was

When I emerged from school to enter the
world outside, I was sixteen

probably chronically unfit. His one saving grace was an inability to drink much alcohol. But then he sold the stuff and probably realised what it could do.

After seeing his doctor Sam went to a heart specialist and was told he had angina. Medically the treatment of heart disease was a lot more primitive in those days. Sam was given a few pills and told to take things easy. For a while he gave up smoking but soon was back to his sixty cigarettes a day. The condition was not helped by business worries and ironically a pioneering medical campaign designed to save lives actually contributed towards Sam's early death. This was a mass radiography scheme to X-ray every single person in the country in a bid to detect the early signs of lung or heart damage. My father, who was always terrified of lung cancer due to his heavy smoking, went off to have his chest looked at with a considerable amount of trepidation.

The first time I saw Sam cry was when the result of his X-ray arrived in a grey envelope. It stated that there was something abnormal about his lungs. To Sam it confirmed his worst fears. He had cancer of the lungs. Later we learned it was an old scar from bronchitis in his youth.

That night he went to bed desperately worried. In the early hours he suffered a massive coronary thrombosis in his sleep and died almost immediately. According to Jewish tradition he was buried twenty-four hours later. He was 59.

DR ROGER BLACKWOOD

It is very sad but from a health point of view Bernard and his father did pretty well everything that was wrong. His father was a kind and generous man, devoted to his family. But kindess also means taking care of your health so that you can stay with your family for as long as you can.

The desolation produced by the death of a breadwinner is shattering. Bernard's father smoked heavily. In the First World War cigarettes had been handed out like Smarties and everyone became accustomed to smoking as part of adult life. Such habits die hard, and Bernard's father was no exception. Later in this book I shall deal with the damage smoking causes to the heart in more detail. Sam clearly ate all the wrong foods which were mostly fried. And again we shall go into diet as a risk factor later. He never saw a doctor to check if he had high blood pressure. He was an ambitious man but took little exercise and was overweight.

The tragedy is that Bernard's father could not have known the risk factors of heart disease. At that time they were hardly known. When Bernard was growing up in Liverpool we realised so little about the dangers of over-indulgence. During the Second World War rationing had made everyone fitter by giving us the right sort of food in roughly the right quantities. Then came the inevitable reaction to this after the war when rationing ended and people grasped the opportunity of tasting richer foods. Bernard's parents were also prompted by the survival instinct believing that feeding a child 'properly' would prevent infection and premature death. 'Fattening up' became quite normal and in the general poverty in the middle classes this was achieved by toast-and-dripping and fried bread for breakfast.

The National Health Service was specifically designed to eradicate meningitis, ear infections, pneumonia, tuberculosis and other devastating diseases which killed many in the prime of their life. But we never thought beyond early middle age and 'fat' babies were considered healthy, getting a person off to a good start in life. There was little concept of actually being able to damage yourself, although even then many diseases such as high blood pressure were blamed on stress. At one stage even syphilis was said to be caused by stress. This is because many businessmen caught it when away from home, 'entertaining' in the evenings and working too hard. Indeed it wasn't until about 1960 when heart attacks were reaching epidemic proportions that we began a more careful examination of what might cause the problem.

What we have discovered since Bernard was a child indicates that he always ran the risk of suffering a heart attack. In some instances these risk factors are unavoidable, like race, sex and age. But if you then add risk factors which are avoidable, like a poor diet, lack of fitness and smoking, then you have someone with too many negatives for his own good.

In this chapter I shall deal with risks which are unavoidable. We have ample opportunity to discuss avoidable risks as we follow the rake's progress of our victim. But if we understand every aspect of the many factors leading to a heart attack then we can take steps to avoid following down the same path.

Bernard and his father are white Caucasians. Many surveys have examined the influence of race and environment upon heart disease and we have statistical evidence that Caucasians run twice the risk of having a heart attack compared with non-Caucasians. Indeed you dramatically reduce the chance of having a heart attack if you are born Japanese rather than being British or American. So race is one risk factor. Minus points for Bernard and his father.

Secondly there's the problem of environment and we have evidence on that as well. A study was made of three groups of Japanese men living in Japan, Honolulu and the States. It revealed that the incidence of heart attacks was double in the USA compared with the other two places. The evidence points to the food the three groups consumed. The Japanese diet in Japan is very different from the American-style diet adopted by the Japanese in the USA. In their native land the people eat large quantities of fish, often raw, vegetables and high-fibre foods. In America they enjoyed large quantities of red meat.

A similar result came from a Yemenite and Polynesian study. Yemenite immigrants to Israel who had lived there for more than twenty years died earlier from heart attacks than those immigrants who were recent arrivals of the same age. Polynesians living in the Cook Islands had a ten-times-less chance of developing heart attacks than Polynesians living in New Zealand.

So as Bernard was born in the western hemisphere, in the industrial northern city of Liverpool, you can add environment as another negative risk factor over which he and his poor father had very little control.

Three other inborn factors are important: family history, age and sex. And sadly we shall discover even more negative risk factors for Bernard. As long ago as 1910 it was realised that some heart attacks run in families. Many factors are handed down from parents to children. For example whether your children have blue or brown eyes depends on the colour of your own. And it is highly likely that Bernard's father handed down his own tendency to heart disease to his son. We

When Bernard was growing up doctors
knew much less than we know now about
the causes and treatment of heart disease

are not sure how or why this happens. We just know it does.
Some people hand on a tendency to high blood pressure or
high blood fats, both of which can lead to heart attacks. Of
course it is not automatic and it would be wrong to assume
that because your father had a heart attack you might as well
not bother to try to avoid one yourself because you are going
to die of heart disease anyway. But if the problem runs in your
family, if the inborn tendency is there, then you MUST make
more effort to eliminate the risk factors which are avoidable:
high-fat diets, smoking, high blood pressure.

For Bernard the picture is getting worse: race, environment,
and the hereditary factor too. Quite a list of negatives. You
wonder how he lasted this long. Now we come to age, which
again none of us can avoid. Age is quite a logical 'inborn' factor
and before examining its influence it is worth looking at a heart
attack in more detail.

The heart is a magnificent piece of machinery. Try inventing
a mechanical pump that keeps going without a breakdown for
seventy years or more and you see what I mean. But it does
have components which are prone to weakness. The basic
process causing heart attacks is the gradual narrowing of an
artery of the heart. Arteries are tubes which carry blood full
of oxygen, sugar and so on, to all parts of the heart allowing
it to contract vigorously. This narrowing process is caused by
deposits of a grey-yellow material called 'atheroma' (roughly
Greek for porridge). Atheroma is made up of cholesterol, other
fats, cells and scar tissue, and is frequently found in the arteries
of the heart.

It is at a point of marked narrowing that a clot will form,
blocking an artery of the heart and causing a heart attack.
Quite why atheroma is laid down in our arteries is unclear,
although evidence has accumulated since the late Fifties. For
example we know from the autopsies of US soldiers in the
Korean and Vietnam wars that the process of atheroma begins
as a teenager and then slowly progresses. As we grow older the
narrowings become narrower and the risk of a heart attack that
much greater.

So, inevitably, there is a deterioration of all our bodily organs
as we grow older. Age is another risk factor over which we
have no control and, while Bernard and his father might have

expected to have a heart attack eventually, their relatively young age to suffer disease owes more to their lifestyles than the ageing process. His father was 59 when he died and Bernard suffered his heart attack at the age of 43.

The remaining unavoidable risk factor which gave both men yet another negative is their sex. If we compare men of an equivalent age with women who have not had the menopause, men far exceed women in the incidence of heart attacks. So men are at greater risk, thereby placing them under an even bigger obligation to deal with the risk factors that are avoidable.

What a tragedy for both men that when Bernard was growing up doctors knew much less than we know now about the causes and treatment of heart disease. Current evidence suggests that the major risk factors are *diet, cholesterol, smoking* and *high blood pressure*, rather than obesity and stress. Under the influence of his father, Bernard, like so many, was on a downward path from the moment he was born. And as he reached manhood the lifestyle he adopted only compounded the risk which can lead to a heart attack.

3. Young at heart

BERNARD FALK

For over a hundred years the *Birkenhead News* allowed the great events of British journalism to pass it by. But in 1960 this old-fashioned weekly paper redeemed itself for a century of insignificance by deciding to employ me. I was grateful. Inspired by my uncle who was a national newspaperman of some note I had set my sights on journalism from an early age. But Fleet Street seemed indifferent to the availability of a 17-year-old school drop-out, so until the *Daily Express* realised what it was missing then the *Birkenhead News* would have to do. It was the start of my rake's progress in a career so fraught with health risks that it should carry a Government warning.

Journalism is not really a profession, more a trade, and a relatively tatty one at that. Its heroes tend to be eccentric low-life drunks. Their idea of paradise is swapping newspaper yarns with one another in a bar that gives credit, and stays open beyond licensing hours. These moments are fun as during the raucous laughter large quantities of drink disappear into bodies rotting from self-abuse. Journalists drink as though in perpetual fear that prohibition is being introduced, which means downing as much booze as you can while it's still available. Very few journalists live long enough to draw a pension. They normally expire early from a disease called 'over-indulgence'. As such journalism and I were made for each other.

The offices of the *Birkenhead News* looked as though they'd been lifted straight out of a Dickensian novel, situated in a grubby side street of a shipyard town which lies in splendid insignificance across the River Mersey from Liverpool. The first tram service in the world began in Birkenhead. It is where cardiologist and co-author Dr Roger Blackwood was 'educated'. But since then not very much has happened. The town has always been Liverpool's poor neighbour—which is really saying something. The citizens of Birkenhead walk around with a permanent look of disbelief on their faces, and so would you if you had the bad luck to be living there. But in spite of that, the local paper initiated me into the ancient art of journalism and I took to its bad and wicked ways with total unabashed enthusiasm.

Next door to the newspaper was a pub called The Free Library, so named to enable a past generation of thirsty reporters to announce that they were 'nipping down to the library' without arousing the suspicion that they were drinking during working hours. When I joined the staff the pretence had long since gone. In fact at the beginning I was the only sober person in the place. And that didn't last long as I quickly became assimilated into the nuances of the job. I have no idea what years of heavy drinking can do to the heart. But alcohol is an occupational hazard with journalists (and doctors) and while it isn't compulsory to become a brain-damaged sot, many do.

Journalists don't just drink because the stuff tastes nice. After enough who cares about the taste anyway? My mother doesn't drink because she says, 'It goes straight to my head'. Mother hasn't realised that's the whole point of the exercise. Drinking is really a social pastime until you become an alcoholic and then only other alcoholics can be bothered drinking with you. But, more seriously, I believe journalists drink too much because at times their job can cause such incredible stress. A drink offers an escape from reality. It's a release or an anaesthetic. Certainly many of the people I worked with on a variety of newspapers were anaesthetised for 90 per cent of their lives and I shall be interested to learn whether a regular intake of alcohol does damage the heart.

Of course, as a young man just starting your career, the last thing you ever worry about is your health, particularly if you feel well for most of the time. I was very ambitious and quickly realised that the *Birkenhead News* did for journalism what the *Mary Rose* did for Henry VIII's Navy.

Eager to scent out international scoops like grisly murder stories, I ended up in charge of the 'hatched, matched and despatched' department: births, weddings and funerals. Indeed I spent a miserable year tramping the streets of Birkenhead gathering news about the humdrum affairs of the local citizens, the only excitement being the occasional car crash, chip-pan fire and the rare phenomenon of Tranmere Rovers football club actually scoring a goal. Fleet Street seemed a million miles away although its representatives on Merseyside hung out—or dried out—in the Liverpool Press Club.

Alas the club itself is no more but at one time it was one of the most entertaining venues in the country, providing you liked drinking, playing poker and the spectacle of grown men behaving like adolescent schoolboys. I adored the place. It was where you met a breed of men I longed to join. They wore bow ties and trilby hats. Their stories were read by millions. They were proper newspapermen who worked for the nationals.

There was Bill, later a famous columnist on one of Fleet Street's biggest selling tabloids. Bill wrote like a dream, and still does, but he spent his life in a perpetual daze trying to figure out where he was. Then there was Jack, a little red-faced reprobate who liked to sleep on the billiard table when his wife chucked him out. I adored all these toe-rags because although their private lives were a catalogue of catastrophes they were superb newspapermen.

Liverpool is a very 'newsy' city. Then it was just about to become world famous due to four young lads called The Beatles who performed rock music at a basement club called The Cavern around the corner from the Press Club. So very often Fleet Street's men on Merseyside wrote the big splash stories which led the front pages of their papers. As for me, I was hooked, not only on the idea of becoming like them, but on their way of life. It was the beginning of a career which put me in Fleet Street myself at the age of 22, but also into a lifestyle which placed me in intensive care twenty years later.

I do not know why journalists should have a wayward existence, but somehow the job leads you to self-indulgence and excess. You live under pressure, working against the clock, trying to meet a deadline. You work long hard hours, pitting your wits against a ruthless and often unscrupulous opposition. Journalists tend to like one another's company. Let's face it, they are probably the only people who will want to mix with their kind. But your colleagues on rival newspapers will do anything to get a better story than you. So the good reporter must be alert, intelligent and resourceful. It might be great fun but it hardly leads to an easy life. Stress, pressure, the spirit of competition, often the worry of survival, creates an individual who is forced to live hard. And it is quite natural that he should want to play hard as well. Hence the drink and why so many journalists end up as alcoholics.

By my early twenties I was working for a national newspaper, as a reporter on *The Daily Mirror*, a good newspaper at that time. Hired in Manchester I spent a year in Dublin discovering that when it comes to alcohol the Irish are in a class of their own, and then I went to the Fleet Street headquarters. I was on the road to the top, successful, single, well paid, almost permanently pissed and physically I was pretty knackered. Life seemed wonderful and who cared then about the damage it might cause?

Naturally I smoked. That had begun when I was about fourteen. Everyone smoked in those days. It was cool, it was fashionable, macho, smart. It was grown up and clever. I started to smoke largely because most of my friends at school smoked in secret. Believe it or not we began by puffing cinnamon sticks obtained at the chemist's and then graduated to Woodies which we bought in fives or singles from the corner shop. In those days cigarettes were cheap and it was a long time before a more enlightened society put public health warnings on cigarette packets or introduced advertising restrictions. Not that the school ignored the problem of smoking. Fingers were regularly inspected for nicotine stains but a pumice stone in the evening got rid of that and I was only caught once. It resulted in yet another bashing with a stick but sadly that didn't break the habit.

For me the smoking habit began because I was easily influenced by boys of my own age. Then of course my father smoked heavily, all his life. No one realised the dangers. Mother has never smoked which may be one reason why she's so well at the age of 83. But school friends pressured you to smoke, a bit like the way drugs are pushed in the playgrounds today. You were regarded as a sissy if you didn't smoke, a wet who deserved to have his face shoved in a puddle. If you

wanted to be a real man then you lit a fag. By my early teens
I was on about twenty cigarettes a day and when I joined *The
Daily Mirror* my consumption had doubled to forty. You could
see me coming for miles, from the cloud of smoke hanging
over my head. I looked like a walking chimney, hooked on
nicotine and the kind of life which I thought was modern,
clever and in vogue.

Let me tease your imagination. Close your eyes and think
of something rather sordid and unattractive. Try to picture a
mess. It is human, just. It stands about five foot eight in its
socks with the holes. It wears horn-rimmed glasses. It has a
large Scotch in one hand, a beer in the other and a fag hanging
out of the corner of its mouth. Beneath its sloping hairy chest
rests a large, round object spilling outwards which passes for
the beast's stomach. Occasionally it draws in yet another gasp
of poisonous fumes which results in a cough and splutter.
Because it is grossly overweight the beast tends to belch a lot.
This immobile tragedy also suffers from wind. The wind comes
out of many places. In short this thing is not nice to be with.
Other newspapermen recognise it. Most of them look the same.
Any resemblance between it and what God designed the human
race to be is purely coincidental. Guess what folks.

It is Bernard Falk. Aged 25.

I am exaggerating a little. I did not drink too much beer,
just Scotch, gin, vodka, wine, rum, sherry, port, or anything
else that was liquid and sent you to sleep with a smile. It was
quite remarkable that the object also considered itself to be
reasonably intelligent. It was about as intelligent as a brick
wall. Tubby, no let's be honest, FAT. Not an alcoholic but with
an incredible capacity for drink. A heavy smoker. Do I really
need a doctor to tell me that all this was ridiculous? I suppose
so, because then it seemed like the normal way to live. The
job brought pressure and stress in one of the word's most
competitive industries. The drink and cigarettes relieved the
inward tension by acting as a release, and even though I could
never have realised it then I already must have suffered from
high blood pressure. Being two stone overweight would have
influenced that.

I ought to say a quick word about food. Newspapermen tend
to eat when they can. They often have to grab a quick bite

It is Bernard Falk, aged 25

in between rushing from one place to another. And traditionally they eat quickly. Either that or they eat a lot. Reporters have expense accounts. Journalists are courted by people trying to 'place' stories. Indeed much of the public relations' industry exists on the premise that if you wine and dine journalists they will write favourably about your product, business or institution. Like politicians journalists love to be wooed and flattered and because so much of the grub is free then there is a grave temptation to make a pig of yourself—hence the object I became.

None of us cared about the sort of food we ate or its effect upon our health. We either did not know or we did not care. On most evenings after a good solid bout of boozing in a pub behind the newspaper my fellow reporters and myself in the lead would stagger into an Italian restaurant to guzzle large platefuls of spaghetti washed down with cheap red wine. Alternatively the Indian curry houses were opening up in London. No wonder I used to spend half the morning on the loo and developed chronic indigestion which I still suffer from today.

It is a very sordid story. Because I felt extremely healthy I always ignored the prospect that my way of life was damaging my health. Other people got sick: not me. I was young, indestructible. I ate what I wanted, smoked and drank and in my profession nearly everyone did the same. We were interested in satisfying our bellies, our thirst and our dicks (not necessarily in that order). And if you had asked me if I was heading for a heart attack then I would have laughed in your face. Of course I was aware that my father had died aged 59. Perhaps a nagging worry that I could go the same way might have lurked in my subconscious. But Bernard Falk was Jack the Lad and I had many more years to go.

DR ROGER BLACKWOOD

Bernard's lifestyle reads like the plot of a disaster movie and I wonder how many young men in their twenties today behave in the same way: pressure, stress, smoking, drinking, obesity, high blood pressure, unhealthy diet?

Of course there is the arrogance of Bernard's so-called indestructibility. 'It can never happen to me.' Notice how he lays the blame for his attitude towards health upon the pressures of his work. So many men absolve any responsibility for health by saying they must work excessively hard to provide the physical comforts for their family which their wives apparently demand. Because they work so hard they justify their smoking, obesity, and lack of exercise as an inevitable by-product. Most men work hard as a matter of pride. And it is a poor excuse to blame the job rather than yourself.

Tragically 200,000 people a year die in Britain from heart disease. Most of them don't believe it could happen to them either and as a race of people we, the British, are our own worst enemies. We are a stubborn race who characteristically ignore advice, and it is worth while spelling out the sheer damage heart disease causes to the country. Already we swallow up a great deal of the gross national product on health.

Let us suppose that in ten years' time an artificial heart becomes freely available and it works. The minimum estimated cost of each one would be about £25,000 per person. If we pay no heed to preventive medicine, if we fail to tackle the root causes of heart disease, then so many people would need artificial hearts that by the year 2000 the cost to the nation could be a staggering £30,000 million. Clearly changing our lifestyles and eliminating risk factors that are avoidable is a more rational priority for us all.

Smoking

First let us deal with smoking. Bernard and his father were both heavy smokers and the influence of smoking on heart disease is considerable. For a long time smoking has been linked to cancer of the lung, and we have ignored its connection with heart attacks. However if you smoke twenty cigarettes a day the risk of a heart attack is four or five times greater than that of the rest of the population.

It is a particularly potent factor in young women and it is very rare indeed to see a heart attack in a woman who is premenopausal and who is not smoking.

In Britain about 40 per cent of the adult population still smoke. In the States, twenty years ago, the proportion of the population who smoked was 53 per cent. By the end of the 1970s this had dropped to 38 per cent. No such drop in figures was seen in this country except perhaps in those of doctors. Curiously a large number of nurses smoke and young girls tend to be the worst offenders today.

We are not really sure what is the dominating reason why people begin to smoke. Perhaps if your hero or heroine smokes you will follow suit. If those around you smoke, particularly your family and friends, you are likely to be encouraged. Both stress release and stimulation are said to be 'benefits' of smoking and once you start it quickly becomes a habit and for the heart cigarettes in particular can be lethal.

When you smoke, whether you claim to inhale or not, the carbon monoxide level rises. Carbon monoxide is the gas which kills people if they put their head into a gas oven. Instead of oxygen going into the bloodstream a significant quantity of carbon monoxide gas enters instead. This damages the lining of blood vessels and may lead to fatty-like material being deposited inside them. In other words it can narrow the passageways through which the blood flows.

In addition smoking can make blood vessels contract, reducing their diameter and thus the flow of blood. The cause of this is nicotine, coupled with the fact that smoking stimulates the production of adrenalin in the body. If contraction of the blood vessels is widespread, blood pressure can be raised.

Recently smoking has been shown to make tiny particles in the bloodstream called platelets stick together more readily. This could result in the final blockage which causes a heart attack. As you smoke your heart may become irritable and produce extra beats. This may not be serious but can be quite frightening. Finally smoking can change the ratio of your blood fats, increasing the risk of atheroma. So what are the risks?

The risk of heart disease is increased particularly in women who smoke and who are on the pill. The risk increases fourfold at the age of 35 and fivefold at the age of 45.

Even second-hand or passive smoking is important. Two studies—in Japan and New Zealand—have shown that the risk of lung cancer is significantly increased in non-smoking wives of smokers, that chest infection is more likely to occur in small children whose parents smoke. It is fair to say that no

direct evidence is available to link heart attacks with second-hand smoking. But breathing in other people's cigarette smoke will not do you any good.
So is it worth quitting? Or for a heavy smoker is the damage already done? Certainly not. Those who smoke twenty cigarettes a day will almost halve their risk after just one year of abstinence. And your chances continually improve as time goes by.
Remember tipped cigarettes carry the same risk as unfiltered cigarettes. When it comes to reducing the risks of heart attacks we cannot compromise on smoking.
Of course to someone who is hooked on smoking, giving it up can cause great discomfort, even distress. The time to try is when things are going well and not during periods of stress. This sounds obvious, but you will rarely succeed if you are constantly worried about promotion at work or something similar. Wait until you have been promoted. Persistence is vital. If at first you don't succeed then don't give up. Quit again.
Nicotine chewing-gum can be a useful aid because it helps to reduce the withdrawal effects of smoking. Establishing a smoking free period in the day and then gradually extending it is sometimes helpful. And keep changing your routine. Many people 'light up' after a meal. Altering the time you eat your main meal of the day can be useful. Also coffee drinking is associated with a cigarette. Change to tea or tonic water. Don't sneer at joining an anti-smoking group because in it each person supports the others. Some people turn to a psychologist for help. If you find it too difficult to stop smoking on your own, your doctor may be able to offer further assistance.
I stress again: smoking is dangerous. It damages the heart. You must stop.

Alcohol

I am having nothing to do with Bernard's liver. That's another department and I have enough trouble dealing with his heart. Clearly the drift towards excessive drinking was part of his process of growing up. In starting his first job he discovered that alcohol breaks down inhibitions. It helps to cross social

barriers and induces a mixture of melancholy and temporary
exaltation ideally suited to a young, inexperienced but ambitious journalist like Bernard.

Because it is so much part of life to so many people in this
country it is hard to criticise anyone who starts to drink. In
moderation it is an enjoyable social pastime. But in excess it
creates appalling misery. One in seven of all hospital admissions
is alcohol-related. The majority of road accidents are caused
by drink. It is a major cause of marital disharmony and child
abuse. Watching someone die of cirrhosis of the liver is one of
the saddest sights of medicine. We know alcohol rots the liver
but what does it do to the heart? And did it have a significant
effect on Bernard's heart attack even though there is no sugges-
tion that he is an alcoholic?

Modest drinking, one or two measures a day, does not harm
the heart, but moderate to heavy drinking can make your heart
muscles very flabby and can show the symptoms of heart
failure. More significantly, even moderate drinking raises
blood fats and that can lead to atheroma: cholesterol and fatty
deposits which can block the arteries of the heart.

In addition drinking raises blood pressure in susceptible
individuals and this too can lead to heart attacks. So although
alcohol is not a major factor in causing heart attacks, excessive
drinking is an important enough risk factor to recommend
taking steps to curb it, particularly for an individual like
Bernard who has enough risk factors in his life already. The
argument most people put forward on behalf of alcohol is that
it relaxes them. The trouble is that this becomes a habit. Many
people, Bernard included, arrive home and pour themselves a
stiff drink as part of a well-established routine. Most heavy
drinkers are probably not true alcoholics but people who have
got their lives to such a pitch of stress that the thought of
living without substantial amounts of alcohol would seem
impossible.

I have to conclude that in Bernard's case his alcoholic
consumption, moderate to heavy for over twenty years, did
play some role in his heart attack, not only because it raised
his blood fats and blood pressure, but because it places him in
a group of people who are prone to smoke, work too hard, eat
anything and avoid doctors like the plague.

Diet

Since early manhood Bernard has always been at least a stone overweight for his height and structure. His father was exactly the same and already during his childhood a pattern of unhealthy eating was well established.

But *what* you eat, your diet, is just as important when investigating the causes of heart disease. Indeed the link between diet and heart attacks grows stronger every year. During the Second World War, for example, the death rate from heart attacks fell in Sweden, Norway and Finland but rose in the United States. The marked deprivations of diet in Scandinavia compared with the USA were all too obvious but the significance of this evidence was not apparent until much later—too late to warn Bernard's father and his family. In fact proper studies trying to link diet and heart disease did not get underway until the mid-1960s and results weren't made known until much later. In one such study—at a mental hospital in Finland —patients were divided into two groups, one eating a normal diet and the other eating a low cholesterol diet. This continued for six years when the groups changed over. The group eating a normal diet changed to the low cholesterol diet and vice-versa. After twelve years the results were surprising. Both the number of heart attacks and the death rate from heart attacks were halved in the low cholesterol group. Other trials in Oslo, Los Angeles and other places in the USA have shown similar results: those groups on a low cholesterol diet were far less prone to heart attacks.

A different way of looking at the influence of diet upon heart attacks is to study the cholesterol levels in different countries and compare this with the heart attack rate. This was done by Ancel Keys in 1970 and his study showed a remarkable correlation between the two factors. In Japan, where only 7 per cent of the population had a high cholesterol level the incidence of heart attacks was markedly less than in Finland where the incidence of high cholesterol was 56 per cent.

However for those who think that it is too late and that their high intake of cholesterol has done its damage, there is encouraging news, for a recent study has shown that *narrowing of the arteries of the heart actually regresses if the patient sticks to a low cholesterol diet.*

The amount of cholesterol in your bloodstream is directly related to the amount in your diet, and vegetarians have a significantly lower cholesterol level than meat eaters. Seventh Day Adventists and other vegetarians have markedly lower blood cholesterol levels, and at least one study suggests they run a considerably reduced risk of a heart attack. And it may not be just that vegetable matter contains less cholesterol, but that *eating* vegetables reduces the level of cholesterol. Eating about half a pound of carrots a day has been shown to reduce your cholesterol level by 11 per cent—no small amount. Drinking ordinary milk does not increase the cholesterol in your body, but drinking skimmed milk certainly *decreases* it.

Most doctors and heart specialists will agree: diet and heart disease are connected. Obesity is associated with high blood pressure, high sugar (diabetes) and high blood fats: all these factors increase the risk of a heart attack. However most studies show that you need to be 20 per cent overweight before any significant risk appears. If your ideal weight is 10 stone you would have to be more than 2 stone overweight before you need to worry about premature death.

If you are overweight *any slimming diet will benefit you,* but if your blood cholesterol is raised you must reduce your fatty intake. In general you should reduce dairy products and increase dietary fibre. Butter, lard and suet should be reduced while increasing margarine. Keep cream and ice-cream down in favour of skimmed or semi-skimmed milk. Eat less red meat (beef, pork, lamb) and more poultry and fish. Cottage cheese is preferable to ordinary cheese. For cooking, the ideal fats are maize and sunflower oils, not dripping. Vegetables, fruit and cereal are excellent and wholemeal bread is better than white bread.

It is not the function of this book to give you a precise diet. There are many such books on the market but these guidelines can produce a commonsense one.

It is not that cream is bad for you, it is just unhealthy if you have too much of it. Clearly both Bernard's philosophy that he could eat just what he wanted, coupled with his palate which had been weaned on fatty fried foods, only increased the risk factors. More significantly it was another negative to add to the many risk factors which already threatened his life. Both his unhealthy diet and his heavy smoking were major risk factors; but combined in the same person the risk was multiplied. In Bernard's case, there were all the other factors too: the inherited risk, race, sex and environment. Blood pressure is likely to be another dominant factor. Bernard's father almost certainly had high blood pressure without realising it. It is difficult to assess whether Bernard himself had high blood pressure when he was younger, but it was certainly abnormally high when I first examined him on the day he suffered his heart attack.

Blood pressure

Blood pressure was first demonstrated by Stephen Hales, about two hundred and fifty years ago. In an experiment which would make the anti-vivisectionists wild with anger he tied a live horse to the ground and plunged an eight-foot brass tube into one of its major blood vessels. Surprise surprise, the blood rose in the tube almost eight feet. This demonstrated the pressure created by the heart in the blood vessels.

Nowadays we measure it by less barbarous means. You blow up an inflatable cuff round the arm and measure the result in millimetres of mercury. There are two figures which you obtain. The top value is the highest pressure reached in your blood vessel and the low value the lowest pressure reached. (At the age of 20, your norm should be 120/80; at the age of 70—160/100.

So how is blood pressure linked to heart disease? If your blood pressure rises within the blood vessels to a considerably higher level than it should, it is thought to crack the surface of the vessels themselves. In these damaged cracks, fatty tissue can be laid down. Subsequently the high pressure may split the fatty lumps and create a blockage by increasing their size. Hence a heart attack.

We don't honestly know what causes high blood pressure in most people. In only about ½ per cent of cases can a cause be found, a cause about which something can be done. In 19–20 per cent, a kidney may be damaged and indirectly this can lead to high blood pressure. However there is little you can do to 'undamage' a kidney, and in the rest of the population, about 80 per cent, there is no abnormality found whatsoever. Excluding the tiny proportion who have a remedial cause we are stuck with treating the remaining 99.5 per cent with no real knowledge of the underlying mechanism. We do know of certain factors which are likely to make the level of blood pressure rise: excessive salt intake, obesity, stress, lack of exercise and alcohol in moderate quantities can all raise the blood pressure by 5 to 10 per cent.

If we reverse these factors we can change a borderline high blood pressure into a normal blood pressure and a moderately high blood pressure into a mildly high one and so on. But changing these factors will not solve the problem of high blood pressure because it is not caused by these factors in the first place. Indeed the majority of patients will need tablets of one sort or another which specifically reduce blood pressure.

How do you know if you have high blood pressure? People often think that if you have headaches, nose bleeds and a florid complexion you are likely to have high blood pressure. One look at Bernard—obese, stressed and red-faced—and you might automatically think he had high blood pressure. Not so. In fact, high blood pressure is often completely symptomless. It is true that it might give headaches and nose bleeds but it does not give a florid complexion. The only way of knowing if you have high blood pressure is to get your doctor to check it. In a recent survey run by the Slough Health Habit, a screening organisation I run in Buckinghamshire, 80 per cent of adults had had their blood pressures checked in the previous five years when visiting their GPs for some other problem. This is too slapdash. When you are an adult, you should have your blood pressure checked annually and later I shall deal with the importance of regular medical screening in more detail.

One of the unfortunate terms for high blood pressure is 'hypertension' which suggests that it is all caused by stress. While stress may temporarily raise your blood pressure, after a trauma like a road accident for example, it is certainly not the cause. So do not be upset if your doctor calls you a 'hypertensive'—it only means your blood pressure is raised.

However in Bernard's case, high blood pressure added yet

another negative. He could not help his high blood pressure, except if it was made worse by being overweight. But had he been regularly screened, then he would have taken drugs to reduce or stabilise his blood pressure thereby reducing one of the risk factors.

Later as we follow the rake on his progress—or his slide into ill health—I shall examine other major risk factors: stress, obesity, lack of exercise and Bernard's failure to see a doctor for the last ten years of his life until he suffered a heart attack.

4. On the road

BERNARD FALK

Saddleworth Moor lies on the fringe of the Pennines a few miles from Manchester. As the wind howled across the gorse and heather, the rain lashed into the grim-faced men peering into the ditch. It was the corpse of a little girl, uncovered after a sharp-eyed policeman noticed a piece of bone from her forearm sticking up to the sky.

We newspapermen huddled together, cigarettes burning for warmth, as the police began to dig into the peat. Children, the bodies of murdered, mutilated, little children were being uncovered, the victims of Ian Brady and Myra Hindley. They called them the Moors Murderers, and like other hardened cynics from the national dailies I wept too as the small bodies were gently lifted from their shallow graves.

Obscene is the only way to describe the nightmare of Saddleworth. I spent several months as one of *The Daily Mirror*'s reporting team and one incident, as a blessed light relief from the strain of covering the story, prompted me to get out of newspapers to begin a new career in television. And you can blame Michael Parkinson for that.

In those days Mike was one of the team on Granada Television's magazine programme, 'Scene at 6.30', a mixed bag of local news and gossip. Its stars, including Gay Byrne, now host of Ireland's famous 'Late Late Show', and Mike Parkinson, were household names across the North of England.

I was standing in a chip shop waiting for a bob's worth and a portion of cod having spent the day on the Moors watching the police search for more bodies. Inside the warm greasy atmosphere the place steamed, and the smell of the frying food was enough to make a ravenous mouth water.

Suddenly the queue turned, as a tall, good-looking man strolled into the shop. It was Mike Parkinson, also reporting on the Moors Murders for his television programme. He too was searching for sustenance but his effect on the crowd was stunning. Romance blossomed instantly for the brassy blonde in a headscarf and curlers serving behind the steaming frier, as Mike, with that strong, manly Barnsley drawl, requested, 'Steak and kidney pie luv, with mushy peas and chips'.

Letting out a tiny shriek she grabbed my arm and placed her red painted lips alongside my right ear. 'It's him,' she whispered. 'It's him, what's on the telly.' Time stood still, the moment when I realised that anyone who could stir up a chippy on a wet night in Lancashire had got to have it made. There and then, with a piece of battered cod in my hand, I resolved to leave newspapers and seek a more glamorous job on television. As such Mike Parkinson, who is now a friend and neighbour in the Berkshire town where we both live, has a lot to answer for.

In the days when I joined the BBC as a reporter on the late evening current affairs programme, '24 Hours', there was a lot happening in the world, and for a young man, keen and ambitious to make his mark on the box, it was one of the most exciting and exhausting times of my life.

There were wars to report in Vietnam, Biafra, the Middle East and, of special significance for me, the violent sectarian divisions of Northern Ireland had exploded on to the international stage. I was hired by the BBC as a roving correspondent on a programme which in those days carried immense prestige and enjoyed large audiences. I suppose what's left of the old 'liberal' tradition of reporting the events of the world can be found on BBC2's 'Newsnight' today.

The presenters of the programme were Ken Allsop, James Burke, David Dimbleby and Ludovic Kennedy and our editor, a radical and campaigning Oxford intellectual, was Anthony Smith, today the Director of the British Film Institute. My fellow reporters included Tom Mangold, still the best investigatory reporter on British television; David Lomax, now presenting 'The Heart of the Matter' for the BBC; and a pushy young girl called Linda Blandford who wrote a bestselling book on the Arab oil sheikhs. Quite a formidable team. But significantly for my own future health, working for television in those days induced enormous amounts of pressure and stress. The work placed incredible demands on our time. For a film reporter, being 'on the road' wasn't so much a job as a way of life, and an unhealthy one at that. We lived out of suitcases in a world dominated by airport terminals, tatty hotel rooms and hire-car desks. Above all life was a series of deadlines. Our enemy was the clock.

'24 Hours' was a newsy feature programme covering the big events of the world. Unlike the news bulletins dealing with the precise facts our reporters were encouraged to analyse, comment and express a point of view. In my first year on television I was away from home for nine months, twice in the United States covering the anti-Vietnam War demonstrations which radicalised American youth. Then to Israel for stories on the Jewish occupation of Arab land following the Six Day War; France, for an election; Romania when Richard Nixon made history by becoming the first American President to visit a country behind the Iron Curtain; then to Peru for an earthquake; and I made films on the escalating conflict in Northern Ireland.

By May 1971 I was a nervous wreck, in the early stages of marital problems which eventually led to a somewhat messy divorce. I was still overweight, a heavy smoker and I drank about half a bottle of Scotch a day. I was sleeping less than five hours a night, rarely waking up without a headache and a nasty taste in my mouth. Furthermore I was in jail.

In journalistic circles it has become a bit of a landmark, the story of how a BBC television reporter ended up on the wrong side of the bars inside the maximum security prison in Crumlin Road, Belfast. But for several months it brought me a considerable amount of personal distress, fear, pressure, and like any other major trauma in life it had its funny moments too.

In the winter of 1970 I was in Ballymurphy, a rambling Catholic housing estate in West Belfast, reporting on the rise of a new organisation which believed that violence could achieve a united Ireland. It was the start of a rise to power of an organisation calling itself the Provisional IRA. Ulster was a familiar stamping ground for me.

I had first been sent to Northern Ireland for the BBC in the summer of 1969 to report on an outbreak of violence between the Protestant and Catholic populations and it was the start of a ten-year association with this sad backwater of British colonial history.

When I arrived in Belfast to report on the rapid rise of the Provos who could have guessed the outcome? My film brought me into direct conflict with the law, the hierarchy of the BBC, and eventually landed me in jail. On the programme we interviewed two men, said to be a 'brigade commander' and 'quartermaster' of the Provisional IRA's Belfast Brigade. There was no doubt that they were authentic terrorist leaders. Indeed they were interviewed by me with their backs facing the television camera to protect their identities. The IRA is an illegal organisation and admitting membership is a criminal offence. After the programme was transmitted one of the men who allegedly appeared was arrested while attending a funeral. He was charged with being a member of the IRA and my film was to provide the prosecution with its evidence.

At first the attitude of the BBC was disgraceful. The people interviewed on the programme had been given a specific guarantee that their identities would be kept secret. When I was called as the main prosecution witness a representative of the Corporation's senior management (now retired) told me to give evidence against the man.

At first the BBC also refused to pay my legal expenses. Eventually a leading article in *The Times* argued that journalists should never betray their sources of information, and the BBC hired a solicitor and a barrister but it all added to the pressure and stress this unhappy episode brought me and my family.

Furthermore we received information from Northern Ireland that the IRA intended to kill me if I gave evidence of identification in court. It placed me in the most appalling dilemma. Clearly I had no wish to see a terrorist released into the community to continue his campaign of violence. I have no sympathy for their methods at all, but the Republican movement is an important element in the conflict of Northern Ireland and journalists have a duty to inform the public about their activities. Withstanding all the pressure from the court and the BBC hierarchy I refused to reveal the man's identity and was sentenced to four days' imprisonment for contempt.

Being locked up on the wrong side of the bars in one of Her Majesty's high security prisons was no laughing-matter but I

managed to find some humour in the situation. I was carried
into jail totally plastered after a rousing send-off party by a
gang of reporters, lawyers and colleagues. I was in such a state
that at first the warders on the prison gates refused to admit
me in case I corrupted the inmates. There I was demanding to
be allowed inside while there were hundreds of prisoners inside
trying to get out. Eventually I was 'banged up' in a cell and
left to sleep it off.

The following morning when I had sobered up one of the
warders suggested that I ought to share a cell with a 'decent
professional man' just like me. My 'educated' company was a
doctor doing many years for allegedly killing off his patients
so he could inherit money in their wills. I was so terrified of
him that I stayed awake at night just in case he decided to
experiment on me.

Being 'inside' is an eye-opener for anyone. Then, as now,
the jails of Northern Ireland were packed with young men
caught up in the continuing conflict within a divided community. I mixed with bombers and gunmen from both the
Catholic and Protestant terrorist organisations and was treated
kindly by all of them, including the hard-pressed warders or
'screws' as they are called. I spent my time during the day
working in the prison garden planting little flowers in tubs.
The night before my release a note was pushed under the door
of my cell. It read, 'Good luck and hope to never see you back.'
The signature was that of a ruthless terrorist leader doing life
for murder. At dawn I walked out of the armour-plated doors
of the jail and went off to a hilarious champagne breakfast with
my BBC colleagues. Ironically the alleged IRA gunman at the
centre of the case was out on bail when I was locked up and
after a few weeks of further legal wrangling the case against
him was dropped.

Eventually between 1969 and 1980 I was to make over sixty
programmes for the BBC on the tragedy of Ulster. But that
episode clearly personifies the type of stress and worry which
a reporter can face when simply trying to do his job.

I am sure that the type of life most of us led when 'on the
road' must have eventually played a part in the deterioration
of my health. It wasn't just the work, which was hard enough,
but the lifestyle the work induced. Throughout the Seventies

as a film reporter on a variety of programmes, '24 Hours', 'Midweek', 'Tonight' and 'Nationwide', we pushed ourselves to deliver good quality programmes from the four corners of the globe and when the work was done we played equally hard in order to relax. With my temperament there was no question of moderation. I loved the life and the job and it never entered my head that it could be damaging my health. To explain, let me take you on just one trip during my life as a television film reporter.

The consignment was to spend two months in the United States reporting on a wide range of subjects but specifically the anti-Vietnam War demonstrations on the student campuses. I travelled with John Penycate, one of the BBC's cleverest journalists who was a producer then, and is now one of the reporting team on 'Panorama'. After a spell researching the assignments in New York we covered the street fighting between anti-War demonstrators and the National Guard in Harvard, Connecticut. Along with the students we suffered the effects of CS gas and mace, a particularly unpleasant 'crowd cooler' which makes your eyes stream for days. Then to Detroit and the Great Lakes for a story on the mercury pollution of the River St Clair by a giant chemical corporation, followed by a trip to Washington for a big peace demonstration. More street fighting, baton charges by the police and another gassing, only this time we were issued with police gas masks which offered some protection. After being manhandled by some young demonstrators who accused me of being a 'police spy' I gave my mask away. Remember all these films were hot news and after filming all day John and I, with a bottle of Scotch for company, would have to sit up in a hotel bedroom at night, writing the script, selecting the interview material and then shipping the programme back to London for it to arrive the following day. In those days satellite broadcasts were expensive and consequently few and far between.

So the slog continued. Four students are shot dead by National Guardsmen at Kent State University, back to Washington for the political uproar which followed President Nixon's escalation of the war into Cambodia. Off to New York again to try and penetrate the underground student movement, including the violent Black Panthers. Back to Washington for an inquiry into the crime wave in America's capital city. At night we cruised with a police squad car around the black ghetto watching the nightly carnage, drug-dealing, knife-murders, robberies, rapes and muggings. A serious crime is committed every minute, and we ended up in the thick of it. To Texas next as the nightmare schedule continued. Three films in the Lone Star State, and then to California for an interview with a film producer, back to New York for another political story and all this crammed into six weeks. I would wake up at six having gone to bed a few hours earlier. I chain-smoked, about sixty a day, and at night we got drunk, hopelessly drunk. Furthermore if I had known what was coming I would have been permanently intoxicated. Maybe an alcoholic haze would have obliterated the horrors we were about to see.

We were back in Texas, in the border town of El Paso alongside the Rio Grande, an unromantic narrow strip of sludge which separates the world's richest nation from one of the poorest, Mexico. The film was about the 'wet-backs', illegal Mexican immigrants who slip over the border at night to try to find work in the States. We had spent the day with the Texas Border Patrol, an armed police force who hunt the half-starved illegals across the desert using helicopters and tracker dogs. A cable from London arrived as John, myself and our film crew sat drinking 'sun-downers' alongside the pool of our hotel (the job has its compensations too). 'Go to Peru,' it said. 'Cover the earthquake.' Fifteen hours later we were in Lima, capital city of Peru, and in the middle of a human tragedy I will remember all my life.

The centre of the earthquake was under the Pacific Ocean, fifty miles west of the Peruvian coastline. It was huge. The shock wave crashed into the thin, flat coastal plain flattening towns and villages in its path. Then it hit the Andes. Gigantic slabs of rock fell off some of the highest mountains in the world. Tons of debris showered on to the villages resting in valleys 10,000 feet up. In seconds they were crushed flat, disappearing under landslides of granite and mud. The earth-quake lasted less than two minutes. Over 50,000 people, largely Peruvian Indians, lay dead, gone as though they had never existed. Then the survivors began to die of their injuries and disease.

When I arrived in the mountains, at a town called Huaraz, situated in a beautiful valley, army paratroopers were burying the dead in great pits. Children, the old, tiny babies, hundreds at a time, were thrown into the mass graves without ceremony, like discarded rag dolls. The smell of decaying human flesh was appalling. It is something you never forget. In a makeshift hospital by the tiny airstrip, surrounded by the magnificent snow-covered peaks of the mountains, doctors were amputating limbs in the open air. After a while the mind numbs with the sheer immensity of what you are seeing. You step over bodies in the street but you cannot absorb any emotion . . . the teenage girl in her white bridal dress, the flowers still in her hair, thrown like a bundle of dirty washing into the mass grave . . . the young parents quietly weeping beside the tiny crushed body of their newly born baby . . . the sight of two thousand bodies piled on top of one another while the bulldozers covered them with earth and lime.

It was too much to digest. We thanked God for the work because a film had to be made and our BBC cameraman, Reg Pope, who was to die of a heart attack a few years later, ran off reel after reel of film. We wrote our scripts in a bar, the one building in Huaraz which had survived the earthquake intact. There was only a candle flickering through the night for company, and a miracle—the bar keep had found a bottle of Scotch.

After two weeks and a number of films transmitted which were given special slots on the BBC, we were ordered home. On the way I experienced what was probably a minor nervous breakdown. We had landed in Kingston, Jamaica, where ten years later I was to be married. After the numbing experience of the last two months I was to spend a few days soaking up the sun on the beach. The location was true paradise: the beautiful warm blue of the ocean, palm trees bending in the light tropical breeze, the creamy white sand of the little bays on Jamaica's north coast. I lay on the beach in a heap and suddenly a severe pain shot through my body and everything fell apart. My hands began to tremble uncontrollably, my whole body ached with pains shooting down from my head and across my shoulders down into the back. Half my body went rigid, the tears streamed down my face. People sitting nearby looked away with embarrassment. I couldn't move or speak. I just lay there, weeping, shaking, incapable of any control. Eventually the hotel porters dragged me up the beach to my room and bed. I stayed there for three days refusing to leave the room or eat.

When a doctor came he could find nothing physically wrong with me. And then as quickly as it came the condition went away. It might have been sheer exhaustion or a nervous collapse. Twenty-four hours later I was home. My wife, Noleen, brought our little boy, Andrew, and baby daughter, Samantha, to Heathrow Airport to greet me off the plane. When I saw the three of them standing in the airport lounge I cried again, but this time with sheer happiness and relief.

Two weeks later I was in Israel reporting the Jewish occupation of Arab lands on the West Bank of the River Jordan. The treadmill had begun again. It went on for nearly fifteen years and I would do it all again. Life with all its ups and downs should be full of rich experience and my time with the BBC granted me that, the good moments and the bad. I have been round the world several times. I have seen the appalling things human beings are capable of doing to one another, in Biafra, the Middle East, in Northern Ireland, and Afghanistan. But it has been a life packed with the extremes of human experience. Indeed if the wanderlust is in your blood you still look at a big jet flying overhead and remember with nostalgia when you were 'on the road'. At least I have seen something of this wonderful world and its people although I shudder to think what so many years of the pressure of meeting deadlines eventually did to my health.

DR ROGER BLACKWOOD

There is little doubt that Bernard could have avoided this stressful time of his life. He could have given up work as a journalist, taken a nice comfortable job growing cabbages, with no pressure at all. He could have avoided the strain of travel, leading a cosy nine to five existence and probably his heart would be in better shape. He might have died of boredom

I have been around the world several times.
I have seen the appalling things human
beings are capable of . . .

instead. There is no point in believing that it is healthier to suppress ourselves. There is little we can do to change the way we are. What is important is to identify ways in which we can change the way we behave. First let us examine something which Bernard experienced for many years. That is stress. Let us judge whether it is dangerous to our hearts and what we can do to help.

Stress

Stress is almost certainly an overrated risk factor. In a study in Slough, it was found that most of the population thought that stress was the major cause of heart attacks. But stress in itself is not a major cause. It is important because of the spin-off effects stress produces—smoking and drinking for example. So before analysing Bernard and his stress, which in his case was clearly excessive, we should look at what we know about stress and its reaction on the heart.

Traumatic emotional events are known to cause sudden death in both humans and animals. We have all heard of someone dying of a heart attack during a spate of fighting in a war zone like the Lebanon and it is not uncommon for people to have heart attacks after receiving the news of the death of a loved one. There is no doubt that Bernard will have had a number of very frightening and therefore very stressful episodes in his life. Fortunately none was enough to kill him but they all add up. The wars, his Northern Ireland experience, prison and the tribulations of travel, all provide either extreme fear or unreasonable tension. A study by Peter Taggart, a consultant cardiologist in London, shows that there are electrical changes which show up on an ECG during peaks of extreme stress. He performed continual electrical recordings on people driving Grand Prix racing cars, parachuting and watching violent movies. This does not mean that any temporary or lasting damage is occurring to the heart but it is evidence that something is happening.

Chronic and long-lasting stress is more of a problem to most of us who will never have such an exciting life as Bernard. The fact that he enjoyed his job so much perpetuates the stress he has been under. In the following list you can see many of the stresses and strains we are all likely to suffer from.

ACUTE STRESS

Death of a loved one
Divorce
Personal danger or threat
Chronic illness of someone close

CHRONIC STRESS

Bereavement
Divorce
Work:
  dissatisfaction
  deadlines
  overload
  change of status (job, financial)
Life events:
  daily hassles
  marital dissatisfaction
  retirement
  building an extension or DIY
  moving house
Financial/Social:
  wrong social grouping
  loss of status (unemployment or redundancy)
  inappropriate education

Bereavement and divorce are self-explanatory stresses which can continue for years. In general it takes about five years to 'get over a divorce'.

Some people never get over a bereavement. Mortality rate in widows is much higher than expected and leads to the 'broken heart' syndrome.

Work and stress are linked in many ways. Overtime work, the repetitive stress of an assembly-line and unreasonable work demands have all been associated with heart disease. Carrying on two jobs at once is also a significant risk factor along with a sudden increase in job responsibility. Deadlines create stress. Taggart performed exercise tests on a group of men just before and just after they were experiencing deadlines. After the deadline they were able to perform much better, or in other words, once the stress was over.

At home there are numerous stress factors as well as the obvious marital problems. Moving house or building an extension is much more stressful than we realise. A burglary or impending retirement can be very unsettling. Keeping up with the Joneses is another problem. Divided religion in a family doesn't help. An upper social class family living in a lower social class also produces considerable tension.

It would seem from this list that we all suffer the most appalling stress and that death might seem just around the corner. But it's not that bad. No Prime Minister has ever died in office of a heart attack. There is no definite proof that stress in itself causes heart attacks and I believe that stress is only a contributory factor rather than a direct cause.

So what happens in our body when we are under stress? Initially we produce hormones, adrenalin and cortisone, as well as stimulating our nervous system. Adrenalin is the 'fight or flight' hormone produced at times of stress as a normal reaction to gearing up our bodies for action. Our breathing increases, the heart beats faster and more strongly, blood is directed to muscles rather than the stomach or gut, our brain is most wide awake. This sounds fine but if you subject your body to this both continuously and excessively you may run into problems. Too much adrenalin is like leaving the choke out on a car all the time. Bernard must be in the top league when it comes to producing adrenalin and I doubt whether he would function properly at all without buckets of it.

High levels of cortisone, another hormone, increase cholesterol in your blood as well as reducing the ability of the body to fight off infection. All these hormones have been associated with high blood pressure and heart disease if secreted in excess.

We all have an automatic nervous system. As far as the heart is concerned, it constitutes the brake and accelerator over which we have no direct control. In a moderately stressful situation, like giving a talk in front of an audience, the accelerator works, speeding the heart, while extreme stress, which can be caused even by visiting the dentist, may cause the brake of the nervous system to work. In simple language, we faint.

Stress, one way or another, affects the heart in a modest

way. A variety of medical studies looking at stress in population groups have shown no convincing evidence of great risk to the heart and so while we must take stress into account we should not assume it is the ultimate risk factor.

So what can we do about stress? Try telling someone like Bernard to take it easy and you would be banging your head against a brick wall. Indeed that could cause enough stress in itself particularly for those who give him advice and have it ignored. People like Bernard thrive on stress and if you take it away he would become frustrated and irritable. As I said earlier, if he had packed up his job with the BBC and taken a boring mundane job that might have been even more damaging to his health.

If stress becomes a problem causing you real anxiety then a doctor can help and you should go and see one immediately. The doctor can offer you pills, although this is less and less common. More likely the doctor will guide you to one of the many 'stress packs' now available or to someone who specialises in stress.

A major cause of stress is ambition but I have yet to meet an ambitious man who admits to it. There is nothing wrong with ambition, after all someone has to be the Chairman of ICI. But many climb up a mythical ladder not really sure of what they are aiming at. They try to get to work before any of their colleagues and leave later in order to impress. But whom? If we can see our destination, then stress may be lessened. *You* may not know what your ambition is but your spouse probably will.

Secondly it is a good idea to work out what is good and bad stress in your life. Good stress makes your work better. It may be writing a report on a subject or just completing a good day's hard physical labour. Bad stress makes you feel unwell. This may be presenting data to an audience or explaining to your wife why you came home late. Clearly you should try to get rid of the bad stress and keep the good stress. It's hard to know what is each type of stress in your life. It may take six months to work it out but it is worth a try. There are two other things about stress—holidays and hobbies. A proper holiday is a good thing but pinching an odd day here and there is not relaxing. Hobbies are worth cultivating a long time before you retire. Relaxation is an art in itself.

Personality

Linked to stress is the concept of type 'A' and type 'B' personalities. As long ago as 1910 it was recognised that personality can be a factor in heart diseases. Sir William Osler wrote: 'It is not the delicate person who is prone to heart disease, but the robust, vigorous and ambitious man, someone with their life always going full steam ahead.'

A typical 'A' personality is someone with excessive competitiveness, aggression, always pressed for time, born with a restlessness, hostility, explosiveness, with feelings of having to struggle against the limitations of time and the insensitivity of the environment. 'A' personalities hate queues and will do almost anything to avoid them.

Guess who is an almost perfect 'A' personality? No prizes. Bernard fits the description perfectly and type 'A' people are more likely to suffer a heart attack than shy, retiring chaps like me who are type 'B'. Indeed the secret category 'A' person hiding inside a category 'B' exterior is probably at greater risk. Bernard is an 'A', an extrovert with an excitable and aggressive nature.

It seems logical that the type 'A' personality produces more adrenalin than the type 'B'. During aggressive questioning for example the type 'A' person produces 30 per cent more adrenalin than the type 'B'. Type 'A's normally have higher adrenalin levels during the day, during exercise, doing an impossible jigsaw puzzle, during competitive games or challenged by some mental arithmetic. This surge of adrenalin can raise the blood pressure and heart rate.

So if this is a risk, then can you change a type 'A' to a type 'B'? I believe it is possible, but it would mean a total change of lifestyle and even a change of environment. Most successful people are type 'A' and would curse you if you changed them into type 'B', and there is no way anyone like Bernard could change his own personality and lifestyle to become someone he clearly isn't. It would drive him crazy and everyone around him too. He was bound to seek a career and a way of life that offered excitement, variety, fun and a challenge. In many ways he would probably prefer to have a life full of variety and pressure even if it meant dying at an earlier age.

Guess who is an almost perfect 'A' type
personality?

More important than trying to change our personalities is the need for everyone, but specifically category 'A' individuals, to realise that they are more at risk and to use the medical service in this country to protect themselves against the danger of heart attacks.

Medical screening

Bernard has told me that during his time with the BBC when he was filming around the world he hardly ever saw a doctor. Indeed on checking he found he had a brief spell of illness caused by an unidentified tropical disease picked up while filming in the Middle East. He had a bout of malaria which he got in Nigeria during the Biafran War and apart from that he seemed to be disgustingly healthy. He must have seen a doctor about three times in nearly fifteen years. This was extremely unwise particularly for someone leading his type of life. Because you do not feel ill does not mean that things are all right. Many problems associated with the heart show no symptoms at all, like high blood pressure.

You feel great but you are not. If Bernard had insisted on a regular medical check-up, obtained either through the NHS, or privately in schemes run by organisations like BUPA, then he could have identified and thus avoided factors which placed his life at risk. Of course you cannot force people to lead a healthier life. There will always be a few who think they are indestructible.

In the United States people are much more conscious of the need for regular medical screening, probably because, as we have said, the cost of being ill in America without the cushion of the National Health Service is a deterrent. But screening can be made available on the NHS in this country. Detecting high blood pressure is important and a chest X-ray will not only enable doctors to see the state of your lungs but whether there are any abnormalities in the size of your heart. A regular blood test offers even more protection.

Many medical practices offer an excellent service for this kind of thing. Some doctors contact individuals or families to remind them of check-ups. The trouble is that many patients find they are too busy to go, which is crazy. Private patients seldom miss an appointment; and if they do, they ring up to apologise. In my NHS clinic at least 10 per cent of patients don't turn up and then expect a repeat appointment. In many ways we think of the family doctor as someone at our beck and call so that health comes into the same category as our regular haircut, a necessity only when it can be squeezed in.

The GP has a crucial role in the health service. The hospital deals with the end-product of disease. Only a GP can prevent it in the first place and many are interested in this problem. Give your GP a chance, give him some encouragement and he will help you, starting with your blood pressure. In my five years as a consultant I have liked every patient I have seen except for the odd one or two. In that time there have been nearly 50,000 outpatients' appointments. I have not yet met a GP I do not like. So given those two facts preventive medicine offers wonderful opportunities to screen patients clearly at risk, not only from heart attacks but many other diseases too.

If every person in the country were to be medically screened, if only once a year, then we could reduce the number of heart attacks. Preventive medicine is the first line of attack against disease and in the Appendix I show how one community in Slough is now teaching schoolchildren to take their own blood pressure and pulse rate in the classroom, while encouraging them to take plenty of exercise and eat healthier foods.

Your doctor can also help you to give up smoking. He will of course inform you of the dangers but will also emphasise the benefits of giving up and give you help to stop. More and more GPs emphasise a proper diet and it is absolutely essential that we know whether your blood pressure is normal or not. If too high then superb drugs are available today which can keep the levels down.

Exercise

Fitness, the all-round general state of your entire body, can have a significant influence on the state of your heart. If you are overweight this can exacerbate high blood pressure. All forms of exercise, providing they don't cause too much physical or mental strain, and are sensibly geared to your age, weight, state of health and general fitness, are beneficial. Bernard hardly ever had any regular exercise, thus adding another risk factor to all the others.

In the 1950s a survey was made of London bus drivers and bus conductors. The drivers sat all day in their cabs whilst the conductors ran up and downstairs. The incidence of heart attacks was substantially higher in the drivers than in the conductors, although it had to be pointed out later that the drivers were fatter. Later, another study, this time among British civil servants, showed that those enjoying vigorous physical activity ran half the risk of dying prematurely compared with those who did little exercise, particularly if they also managed to avoid getting fat.

Of course it could be argued that people who do not take vigorous exercise would be unlikely to know they had heart disease until it was too late and that this would bias the results. But a famous twenty-two-year-long study of San Franciscan long-shoremen showed that the harder the physical work you did, the less likely you were to have heart disease. There are many other studies giving similar results proving a link between exercise and lack of heart disease, but it is not all that strong. We know that even marathon runners in training can have a heart attack. It is fair to say however that if you do take regular exercise you are more likely to take care of your health in general, and both stop smoking and eat the right diet.

It is clearly impossible for a busy businessman, workman, or busy journalist like Bernard, who now lives a sedentary life, to take as much exercise as a San Franciscan long-shoreman. Nor is it advisable to go out and do vigorous exercise, like squash, without first talking to a doctor. An unfit middle-aged man who suddenly decides to have a game of squash runs a substantial risk of sudden death. Squash is an excellent game if played regularly, say three times a week, but for most of us a period of twenty minutes, three times a week, doing modest exercises—say walking, swimming or cycling—is about right. What about jogging? The thought of Bernard jogging fills me with horror. I can imagine him collapsing on the spot. You should not contemplate jogging without a chat to your doctor first, particularly if you are middle-aged and overweight. Jogging is an excellent pastime if you enjoy it but I have never seen a jogger smile as he runs. And I believe jogging does carry risks. Statistically there is a definite mortality associated with jogging and a significant number of accidents (twisted or broken ankles, dog bites, road accidents, muggings etc.). So do not take up jogging because it is the 'in-thing'. There is no absolute proof that exercise will prolong your life so common-sense is all important. Joggers who run five to six miles per day often become depressed and irritable if they don't run. It is rather like a drug withdrawal effect and there is good biochemical evidence for this. Perhaps this is why joggers become so passionate about their sport.

Rather than flogging yourself half to death by jogging or running around as a middle-aged, unfit and overweight member of a squash club, it is better to work out a sensible exercise programme for yourself. Daily exercise, even for ten minutes in the morning or before you go to bed, is a far better idea and is more likely to become part of your life. You should walk upstairs rather than take the lift. Park half a mile away from work and walk. At lunchtime walk a fairly brisk mile. Three times a week either walk, swim or cycle for twenty minutes as a separate exercise. We are only just beginning to be more health conscious in this country. It is certainly worth a try and I only wish during the particularly busy time of his life while working 'on the road' for the BBC that Bernard had taken regular exercise. As well as all the other risk factors his lack of exercise was yet another danger to his heart. But in addition to all the foregoing factors, Bernard fits into yet another category which, although a minor factor in assessing heart disease, is yet another risk.

Social class

Perhaps the most intriguing of all minor factors is the influence of social class. In theory professional people like doctors and lawyers are social class 1. Unskilled labourers are social class 5. But take a look at Bernard—when he speaks he sounds like social class 5 but his luxury house equipped with swimming pool he hardly ever uses, and flashy sports car look like social class 1.

His job, journalism, one might call semi-skilled labour, i.e. social class 3 or 4, even though most journalists make the mistake of believing they are in a professional class. So it is difficult to place Bernard in any significant category, particularly as most journalists feel equally at home with dukes and dustmen. However it is interesting that in men the incidence of heart attacks is higher in social classes 4 and 5 than 1 or 2. The idea that it is the business executive who is particularly at risk is wrong. Heart disease attacks all classes in our society but increasingly those who might call themselves 'working class'.

Several facts about class are important. Fewer people in social class 1 now smoke. The risks of smoking seem to have penetrated the understanding of the more affluent, better educated professional classes. Perhaps it is simply that when it comes to health factors they are more 'aware'. From experiments conducted in Slough it was clear that there was much more eating of brown and wholemeal bread in social class 1 than social class 5. The inference is that social class 1 is more aware of the need for a healthy diet. Certainly the move towards health foods—fresh fruit and wholemeal toast for breakfast—has not replaced the working man's fried bacon, eggs, sausage, and fried bread soaked in animal fat. There is nothing snobbish about this. Most of us love the traditional British breakfast as well. But not every day. At the very most once or twice a week.

An interesting study in the United States looked at social support and found a much higher incidence of heart attacks in those with a low number of social contacts with spouse, friends, or the church. Clearly the influence of others around you plays a role. Drinking is a social activity and only the serious alcoholic prefers to drink alone. On the other hand, it is easier to give up smoking if not surrounded by smokers.

Risk test

So how do you assess your own risk? Your *diet, smoking* and *high blood pressure* are the major risk factors. Bernard ate the wrong food and in excessive quantities which is why he was overweight. He rarely took exercise, he smoked, and consequently these factors combined to give him high blood pressure. Any combination multiples the risk if they occur together in the same person.

It is possible to discover your own risk factors and I suggest everyone uses this as an exercise. It could identify the dangers of your own lifestyle. You can follow the questionnaire on p. 74 and add up your score. You will have a clear idea of what you are. However, you will have to visit your doctor for a blood cholesterol and blood pressure measurement.

Whatever your score (Bernard's was 21, mine was 5!) the major problem is what to do about your own risk factor, and while I have offered some indication—giving up smoking, regular medical screening to assess blood pressure, diet, exercise—I show in the Appendix how a community can help itself. In the meantime we are forced to watch Bernard move from a lifestyle of moderate danger into very high risk indeed.

What a good chance to learn from his example and try to avoid making the same mistakes.

THE RISK TEST

			score
1. Do you smoke	40 cigarettes a day or more?		7
	21–40?		5
	11–20?		3
	1–10?		1
	0?		0
2. Is your cholesterol level	4.5?		0
	4.5–5.5?		2
	5.5–7.0?		4
	7.0–9.0?		6
	9.0?		8
3. Is your blood pressure (lowest reading)	120?		4
	110–120?		2
	90–110?		1
	90?		0
4. Is your blood pressure (highest reading)	200?		4
	160–200?		2
	140–160?		1
	140?		0
5. Are you	male?		1
	female?		0

6. What is your weight in kilograms?

   What is your height in centimetres?

   Now calculate: $\dfrac{\text{Your weight in kg x 1000}}{\text{Your height in cm}^2}$

   If your answer is more than 2.75 2

   If less than 2.75 0

7. Has any of your immediate family (father, mother, uncle, aunt, sister, brother) suffered a heart attack under the age of 55?

   Score two points for each member:

		score
	1	2
	2	4
	3	6
	4	8
	5	10

Total score _____

SCORE
0–5 = low risk
6–9 = moderate risk
10–15 = elevated risk
16 and above = high risk

5. Suicide is painless

BERNARD FALK

In 1978 I thought it would be quite nice to become a millionaire. Eight years later I still think it's a pretty good idea but I am more concerned with avoiding bankruptcy and listing the milkman as a major creditor. Going 'into trade' was a significant period in my life if you consider the added strain, pressure and worry that becoming a businessman entailed. I am not suggesting that businessmen are any more at risk from heart attacks than labourers but they seem to face greater risk factors when it comes to avoiding problems with the heart.

Compared with people who do manual physical jobs the business community takes less exercise. They drink more, eat too many expense-account lunches and tend to suffer more from stress. Furthermore those factors add obesity to the number of risks and this in turn leads to high blood pressure and yet further strain on the heart. If that wasn't enough the sheer excitement of business, like winning the big contract, can introduce huge amounts of adrenalin into the system. That is all right in small doses, but dangerous if it happens regularly over many years.

Some time ago I met a business tycoon who had built up one of the world's great business corporations. He was thin, fit and he neither smoked nor drank alcohol. But when excited his face went a bright red and his eyes literally popped out of his head. To emphasise a point of view he would shout and thump his hand down on his desk. Confronting this apparition of energy was a frightening experience and I was not surprised when I learnt that he had dropped dead of a heart attack. This chap had acquired great wealth and was blessed with a happy devoted family. He was only 58. But he oozed astonishing amounts of nervous vitality and had literally blown himself up with excitement. He probably had high blood pressure and was far too busy making millions to see a doctor even when he felt ill.

My ambition, though a driving force, has always been a bit more modest. I became a businessman largely because I found myself obliged to increase the personal wealth of my first wife's lawyers. Eight years ago I was still working as a relatively lowly paid reporter with the BBC and going through a divorce.

It would be unfair to lay any blame on the first woman mad enough to join me in holy wedlock. We still live near one another which is handy when I get Securicor to deliver her maintenance payments in the armour-plated truck.

But to be serious for a moment, although it was largely my fault that the marriage did not work, most people who have suffered a divorce will understand the pressure and anxiety that such a traumatic event can cause. There is nothing worse than a divided family and the guilty party can suffer just as much from the stress as an innocent partner.

Thankfully my ex-wife and I still speak to one another and I see my three beloved children from that marriage very regularly indeed. But I was flat broke after the divorce. My first wife's lawyer worked for an old traditional legal firm called Plasma, Plasma, Leech and Takehimforhisshirt Associates. Due to her lawyer's desperate intent that I should finance his new Rolls Royce, ocean-going yacht, country mansion, and holiday in the Bahamas, I was forced to increase my earning power.

After the divorce settlement I added up what I had left. There was plenty of room in the haversack but I couldn't afford the crisps. It only goes to prove that when Shakespeare said, 'Sweet are the uses of adversity', the old fool wasn't going through a divorce. Hence my need to start a business.

I looked around for an easy way to make money, like becoming a Conservative MP, trade union leader or common criminal, but the prospects looked decidedly bleak. Fortunately the BBC helped to provide the answer. I was asked to make a series called 'Captains of Industry', a profile of half a dozen successful British companies and the men at the top who ran them. During the filming the chairman of one major concern conducted himself rather badly during the interview. He stumbled, seemed unsure of his facts and gave a very poor account of himself. It was strange because off the television camera he was bright, articulate and entertaining.

Later it occurred to me that you could make money training people like him to appear on television: something that is second nature to TV professionals, like Arthur Scargill or Margaret Thatcher, but an art to be acquired by most members of the business community. So my company was born. And like most small businesses Falkman Limited began as a very tiny sprat indeed.

I set up shop with my second wife, Linda, sharing a borrowed desk, in a borrowed corner of a borrowed office, in a borrowed building next to a Soho massage parlour. You could come and book a television training course with us or go next door to have your plonker rubbed. But much to my amazement the business enterprise began to prosper. We actually started to acquire clients and much to my surprise they paid us. The first year's turnover was £15,000 and we added to the services we could offer the business community by branching out into video. It was the start of the video revolution in communications, using television to help companies sell their products and communicate internally with one another.

We make video programmes for training staff, to sell goods in shops, at exhibitions, even to convince shareholders during a takeover bid in the City that they should back a particular management team. Soon we had built up a list of major international clients. Today a dedicated and hard-working professional staff of video and film writers, researchers and producers work for our company, and we achieve a turnover of considerably more than a million pounds a year. A year ago I formed another production company in the town where I live, with television presenter Frank Bough and a local businessman. Together we have built up a sound, successful business, and it has all become worth while . . . unless you count the damage it might have done to my health.

At the beginning it was not possible to abandon my work for the BBC entirely. Most of my wages went to my first wife and it wasn't really a fortune for her to keep three young children, and her lawyers, all on her own. So with a second wife and another family due—suicide is painless—I found there wasn't enough money left to feed a church mouse never mind half the neighbourhood. Also if you take out large wages yourself from a new business then very quickly it is drained dry and people have to be made redundant. I was determined to give my company time to grow. Therefore I ended up doing two or three jobs at once. It wasn't very long before I found myself on another nightmare treadmill of work, work, even more work, so that from one day to the next I never really knew if I was coming or going.

Having for years found it difficult to snatch more than five hours' sleep a night, I now find that I don't want more. Working as a reporter with the BBC, running a business, writing for various newspapers and presenting a BBC Radio 4 holiday programme called 'Breakaway' each Saturday morning, guaranteed that I had no time to sleep more than five hours a night whether I wanted to or not.

I also have a phobia of traffic jams, just as I have of queueing. Only the British, the Americans and the unfortunate people living in Communist countries tolerate queueing. Queues were invented by politicians to keep the peasants in their place. The French managed to banish queues from their culture during the revolution. In those days there was nothing worth queueing for. So nowadays the French do not queue. They just push people over instead.

But as I struggled to fit so many commitments into so little time the pressure began to build up. I live twenty-five miles from my office in London. It has always meant driving to work each day, down a motorway which resembles a gigantic parking lot during the rush hour. So I used to get up incredibly early to leave my home at 6.30 a.m. Of course I could have gone by one of British Rail's luxurious commuter trains but believe the sheer joy of that should be reserved for a person who likes walking through snowstorms totally naked while whipping themselves with barbed wire, as a pack of angry baboons stamp on both feet with hob-nailed boots (if you get my general drift).

So take a typical day a few years ago. Up at 6.00 a.m. for a quick fag and a cough. No time to drink the coffee so carry it with me in the car. Six-thirty a.m. a mad 100 m.p.h. dash down the M4 praying to beat the traffic. At 7.30 a.m. deal with my letters and write video scripts for my company. A radio programme to record at 11, and off to BBC television to record a film script. Lunch is a business extravaganza. I work hard, so play hard. Big steaks, lots of wine, cigarettes between courses, a cigar at the end. Between 3 p.m. and 6 more business meetings, a new script to write, and problems to sort out with the staff. A minor detail that, like finding enough cash to pay their wages. At 6.30 p.m. the last meeting of the day and the first Scotch, followed by half a bottle. Leave for home at 8 p.m. taking the whisky with me to sup on the way. Home and another big dinner, several brandies and collapse in a heap at 11 p.m. Don't laugh. It happened day after day for years.

How could I know that my body was about to quit, that like any machine you can push it only so far and then something will have to crack? Business merely fulfilled the sheer pleasure I extracted from everything I used to do. I never felt ill, just exhilarated, but then I have the kind of nature that never does things by halves.

My inability to sleep more than five hours must have been due to the sheer weight of so many things on my mind. The trauma of a divorce followed by the strain of establishing a new business while engaged in half a dozen other time-consuming activities must have damaged my health. And God only knows what 'going into trade' was doing to my heart!

It kept ticking but it was competing against a clock, and time was running out.

DR ROGER BLACKWOOD

In many ways this part of Bernard's life demonstrates that stress can be devastating. He is naturally very gifted at his job and is amusing to be with. In other words he's quite an intelligent and amusing chap except when it comes to the common-sense business of looking after himself.

He has followed the classic three 'A's of private business:

> Availability
> Affability
> Ability

He has been very successful and on paper I suspect he is even a millionaire, but ambition begets even greater ambition and there is no doubt he has been determined to get to the top no matter what this frantic lifestyle must have done to his health. Of course if you ask him about this he will deny it. This ambition is a major stress factor in many businessmen leading to overloading of work. People like Bernard deliberately pressure themselves with deadlines. They take on too many jobs at once and they get irritated by all those around who cannot function at the same speed.

Our perception of stress is very individual. Some can take a lot and others very little. Bernard could obviously absorb vast quantities although eventually it even got to him. And let us look at how he did try to avoid the stress and pressures affecting him—by smoking and drinking alcohol. As you drink more your liver gets better and better at getting rid of alcohol so you have to drink even more to get the same effect. This is all right up to a certain point until the liver gets sick of all the overtime it is doing and then it begins to go on strike.

So for Bernard work was becoming overwhelming. Many people cope at this point, just about, as long as their home life is secure. In Bernard's case he was staggering through a divorce. It might have been his fault but his home life became a constant source of anxiety. It has been clearly shown that those without proper emotional support are more likely to have a heart attack and Bernard was adding to the stress in his life.

We have mentioned stress and its effects upon the heart but it also creates a mild inward depression and that amongst other things leads to insecurity and lack of confidence. Bernard added to the stress he was suffering at work by going through a divorce and a second marriage which put even greater financial demands upon him because he had to keep two families.

Bernard became a man swimming in adrenalin. Your stress hormones normally reach a peak soon after 9 a.m. and stay reasonably high, dropping in the evening to a low between midnight and 4 a.m. This is called a 'circadian rhythm' which during periods of extreme stress is lost because your hormones are permanently high. You thus become unable to sleep properly and normally not for long. As stress builds up things which are normally just irritating, like traffic jams, become intolerable; likewise trains, because you normally have to wait

I deliberately walked a tightrope between a
healthy life and neglect

for them, particularly if you're an unfortunate commuter in Britain.

Against this background of stress it is impossible to consider giving up smoking which, like all intelligent people, Bernard knew was bad for him. He also had no time to see a doctor to have his blood pressure checked and could not be bothered with the intricacies of his diet. Once a businessman is at home, decisions of an apparently trivial nature become almost impossible for him to make.

I cannot blame Bernard for not bothering about his health. He was being so successful and was so exhilarated that his mind could not turn to the possibility that something other than his daily pursuits might halt his progress. This is true of so many people—which is why we have written this book.

6. The home straight

BERNARD FALK

I knew that there was something wrong at least six months before I had the heart attack. Tragically I did nothing much about it. I ignored the warning signs and to be honest doctors who examined me also failed to spot the early symptoms.

For me it started when I began to notice a very faint pain in the left side of my body. It was a bit like a muscular ache located somewhere deep inside the rib cage, stretching into the left shoulder, spreading down the left arm. It would last about two or three minutes. It was irritating, rather than causing any real distress.

I began to associate the pain with smoking. Years earlier a doctor had told me that an excessive influx of cigarette smoke could cause the heart to contract, creating a spasm of pain. Naturally because I am more brilliant than any doctor and should be awarded the Nobel Prize for Gross Stupidity I ignored his advice.

But this time, as I rubbed my left shoulder, I thought HEART. I suppose after so many years of neglecting my health I always accepted that one day, if illness was going to strike, then it would involve the heart. Remember my father had died of a heart attack thirty years earlier so the odds were against his son going off to the happy hunting grounds due to an ingrowing toenail.

So I suspected a heart problem when I made a very rare trek to see my GP in the village near my home. He is a decent man and proficient, and the fact that he failed to diagnose a heart problem at the time is something of a mystery. He examined me. He rightly advised me to give up smoking. My heart seemed normal and so was my blood pressure. In fact apart from these slight twinges of pain I felt disgustingly fit.

It was the first time I had consulted a GP for nearly ten

years. I remember feeling how depressing and unhealthy the surgery was. 'Sick' folks sat waiting their turn, coughing and spluttering all over the place and spreading their nasty germs to 'healthy' individuals like me. Having established that there was nothing wrong with me—'a frozen shoulder,' said the Doc —I resolved to stay away from doctors for as long as I could. I would grow old and die without them at the age of 103.

Yet the doctor had offered me one excellent piece of advice. He booked an appointment for me to have an ECG and an X-ray at a local hospital. The ECG is an electrocardiogram which monitors the performance of the heart. He also stressed that anyone over the age of 40 should undertake both examinations once a year.

I was a little frightened, due to years of neglect I suppose, and what they might find inside me. 'Perhaps it would be better not to go,' I thought to myself. Indeed I never showed up for the tests, carrying around the appointment cards for weeks until I eventually threw them away. Had that been an end to the matter I would only have had myself to blame for what subsequently happened.

But a new element of risk had entered my life. I had taken up flying as a hobby to fulfil a childhood ambition. Once I began travelling around the world in big passenger jets then I lost the urge for a while but, determined to find some way of relaxing at weekends, I had enrolled at a flying club for a course of lessons during the summer of 1985. It was superb fun. Some men collect stamps to relax, build models, play snooker, do the gardening. My way of 'taking things easy' was to fling a single-engined light aeroplane around the sky while a terrified instructor attempted to teach me enough to stay alive. Landing was a particular weakness, especially forced landings in fields, as I clocked up the hours above the beautiful Oxfordshire countryside.

Eventually I went solo, a thrill you never forget. Much to the astonishment of everyone and the total horror of the cows grazing in adjoining fields, I took the controls of a Cessna 152, completed one successful circuit around the airfield and made a perfect three point landing. Later I drove my car into a ditch following the traditional 'going solo' celebrations.

But the point of this is that in order to fly in sole command of an aeroplane you must take a stringent medical. It is carried out by doctors approved by the Civil Aviation Authority. I went along for my examination and quickly discovered why the public should feel safe when a British pilot is at the controls. The CAA doctors peer into everything, even up your bum. The medical is extremely thorough, and a good job too when you consider the terrible responsibility pilots have for the safety of their passengers and the poor sods on the ground.

This doctor established that I had the basic requirements of a pilot, like two eyes, a couple of ears, hands, legs and so on. I was given a chest X-ray and an ECG. I remember thanking my lucky stars that I was to have the test which required me to lie on a couch instead of monitoring me on a treadmill. It was normal. Everything was normal, including the urine test which was a miracle when you consider my daily alcohol consumption. However there was one significant exception. When the doctor took my blood pressure he looked anxious. My heart sank. You know what it's like when a doctor does something to you and then seems worried. You imagine you're about to drop dead. 'Your blood pressure is higher than it should be,' he said. 'I am going to take it again.' I told him that my GP had taken my blood pressure a few weeks earlier and it had been normal. 'We have higher standards for pilots to meet,' he replied. Fortunately, or maybe tragically as things turned out, the second time the blood pressure offered a more acceptable reading.

'Lose half a stone and give up smoking and your blood pressure will be A1,' he advised. I promised to diet and abandon the fags (where had I heard that before?), and he gave me a CAA medical certificate approving me fit to fly a light aeroplane. I walked out feeling very pleased with myself.

And so I tried. I abandoned cigarettes and took up smoking little cigars instead. I kidded myself that I had packed up smoking, that cigars were not so dangerous. Of course I totally ignored the fact that I was inhaling over thirty cigars a day. In reality I was probably doing more damage. There is only one way to give up smoking. Stop. It is hopeless trying to cut down, or cadge drags off other people instead of buying them yourself. The only way is to stop totally. It is hell, but only for a while. You never quite lose the craving, particularly on social occasions or after a meal. But gradually the longing diminishes. Surely you don't need a heart attack like me before you are terrified into kicking the habit for good?

However, last autumn, with the CAA medical certificate under my belt to show there was nothing wrong with the old ticker I carried on my lifestyle even more convinced that while other human beings got ill and died I was indestructible, immortal, likely to live for ever. Furthermore that pain in the chest had disappeared. Two doctors had examined me. I was as fit as a fiddle.

Hong Kong offered a welcome diversion from the strain of business in May 1986. I had never explored the colony before and a manufacturing company had offered me a well-paid week there as a media consultant during an international seminar. Luckily my radio programme, 'Breakaway', was interested in a show from Singapore so it offered a chance to kill two birds with one stone. It nearly killed me into the bargain.

For one week I spent eight hours a day in a hotel room packed full of cigarette-smokers lecturing businessmen on how they should handle television interviews. As I have said, one of my companies specialises in training people how to appear on television. I happily puffed away at my thirty-odd cigars a day while inhaling the fumes of cigarettes from the other delegates. At night we were entertained royally by our hospitable Hong Kong hosts, eating superb ten-course Chinese meals full of exotic spices. Naturally I gulped down my normal quota of booze, and as I finally stumbled into bed in the early hours of the morning so my normal intake of cigars and alcohol went up. There was nothing abnormal about this. I had been doing the same for years.

I arrived home knackered. The seminar had been extremely tiring in itself and the entertainment lavish. I felt as though I never wanted to see another spare rib, sweet-and-sour prawn, bowl of rice or bean sprout for as long as I lived (which could have been a short enough time in itself). Furthermore I travelled first class from Hong Kong which enabled me to sample all the lavish hospitality of Cathay Pacific Airways entirely free of charge. I made a pig of myself and by then was not only puffing away at the cigars but at cigarettes as well.

I might smoke twenty cigars a day, perhaps
I do drink too much and work too hard
under pressure . . .

What a mess. But then again I had been doing the same for years.

The pain arrived. I cannot exactly say when, the time and place are lost to my memory. It was in the same spot as the last time, when I had first consulted my GP. But now it ripped into my body as though tearing my chest apart. For a week after arriving home from Hong Kong the pain would come and go. It was unpredictable except for the morning when I woke up: a sharp stabbing pain, deep inside the chest, spearheading a shooting ache into my shoulder, down the arm until it reached the tips of my fingers. It lasted about five or ten minutes and then as suddenly as it arrived the pain went away. It is quite remarkable that a heart patient can feel wonderful one minute and in agony the next. That's why it is so frightening. There is no time to brace yourself, and of course because the pain is so acute you think you are going to die at any minute.

There were so many indications that there was something wrong with my heart. But this deceitful pain was determined to escape identification. It never came with exercise. Too easy that. It might point to the heart. It was at its most severe after a heavy meal. Cunning that. It would mislead the doctors beautifully. It arrived, this pain, like an executioner whom the tortured victim learns to love, when I was tired and drunk. What subterfuge. How clever to dodge proper diagnosis. My pain masqueraded as a digestive problem. It was so successful that a number of doctors were easily taken in.

On a Sunday afternoon after the normal thrash down at the pub and an orgy of roast lamb, spuds, and apple pie, the pain tore into my chest leaving me gasping for breath. The heart was trying hard enough to establish there was something wrong. The right side of my body went rigid. Lying down was agony. It felt easier standing up. Only this time the pain cheated me by refusing to go away. I am sure that everyone has their own level of tolerance to pain. You can suffer for so long and then suddenly you lose control. My pain had always played by the rules. Ten minutes of suffering Bernard and then I'll go away. Walking around the study, shut off from the rest of my family, I kept looking at my watch. God I wish I had called an ambulance. In hospital they would have known what the pain was trying to say. Ten minutes, fifteen, twenty, surely it will go in a moment. Twenty-five, thirty. 'This isn't fair,' I shouted out aloud. 'Go away you bastard, please go away.'

Two hours later I reached almost complete collapse. In fright and desperation I rang my doctor's surgery. It might seem silly to have waited so long but, remember, I rarely saw a doctor and it felt like a climbdown when I made the call. A woman GP arrived. It was sod's law. Just as she rang the bell the pain went away. I felt like a phony, bringing the doctor out on a Sunday evening. And worse, far worse, she could find absolutely nothing wrong with me.

True, it was a cursory examination. Unlike cardiologists GPs rarely carry around portable ECG machines. But she listened to my heart, checked my pulse and took my blood pressure and found nothing really abnormal. The blood pressure was high but she put that down to several hours of distress. Oh! what a victory for the pain. She diagnosed a digestive problem, possibly a hiatus hernia, often found among people who are overweight. She left, promising to fix me up with an examination of my digestive system later in the week.

For the next few days the pain disappeared. There was an occasional twinge, or throbbing ache, but never very severe. On Friday 30th May (you tend to remember dates like this) I went to a local hospital for a barium meal. This is when a patient suspected of a digestive problem drinks an unpleasant substance which is observed radiologically as it passes through the system. To my intense relief this revealed that I was suffering from a hiatus hernia. The doctor advised a more sensible diet.

Yet another examination had failed to disclose any problem with my heart. I left the hospital in excellent spirits determined to have one last fling, a decent meal, a few drinks and a fat cigar to celebrate. The pain in my chest had gone. I felt like a million dollars.

Inside me a blood clot was cutting off the supply of blood to my heart. Part of the muscle which pumps the blood around my body was about to be destroyed. I was in the early stages of a heart attack.

It was nearly going to kill me. It would damage my heart for good. I would never be the same again.

And on that Friday lunchtime I went off to get pissed.

DR ROGER BLACKWOOD

It would be inappropriate for me to comment on Bernard's medical condition before I was called in to examine him on the day he suffered his heart attack.

Bernard had been suffering from a number of chest pains before the actual attack. Were the warning signs missed? It is easy to say that they were, in retrospect. We all make mistakes, and I have certainly made my share with patients who have chest pain. It is often notoriously difficult to make a diagnosis and Bernard definitely does have a hiatus hernia. Many of his pains were related to eating and there is no way every chest pain could be referred to a specialist. In Britain we are short of resources. For example, as a cardiologist, I am solely responsible for one district in Buckinghamshire. There would be eleven full-time specialists in a district of a similar size in the United States.

Medicine is in the habit of kicking you in the teeth as soon as you think you have got it right. Doctors get very upset when they make any mistake, which in part may account for the high alcoholism rates among doctors, and they also have high suicide rates as well. Another factor in Bernard's case was of course himself. He is not the easiest person to deal with. The thought of telling him it might have been his heart would fill one with dread.

A doctor intensely dislikes giving bad news, particularly to one so vibrant as Bernard and there is a great desire to find a suitable alternative diagnosis to explain the situation.

Bernard might well have had a heart attack in any case, even if his condition had been properly diagnosed when he first suffered the pain. Do not be put off by Bernard's experience. It is important to know the symptoms of heart problems which can be identified by patients, family and friends. The objective is to make us all more aware of the warning signs. After all an early diagnosis could prevent a heart attack.

We all know of friends or acquaintances who have suddenly 'dropped dead' with no apparent warning. In a majority of cases this is caused by a heart attack, and the question always arises as to whether there were any warning signs. With the benefit of hindsight someone close to the patient, a husband or wife or close relation, recalls some 'indigestion' or similar symptoms which may in fact have been pain coming from the heart. Usually most patients who have had a heart attack can recall some symptoms during the months or weeks before the episode. Clearly this happened to Bernard. The very fact that these symptoms are ignored confirms their vagueness and, if we visited the doctor every time we had any symptoms, the GP would become an overworked wreck, and the patient a hypochondriac. It is nonetheless sensible to know what symptoms to look out for particularly if you think you are a person 'at risk'.

An attempt to avoid disaster in these people 'at risk' is the annual medical check-up which I have already mentioned. Available privately, it is also often a perk in companies. Alternatively your GP can usually offer this check-up provided he is given sufficient notice. At this annual medical a history will be taken, in some modern surgeries by computer. Then there is a physical examination followed by blood and urine tests, a chest X-ray and an ECG.

All this seems sensible, but does it make a difference? A great value of medical screening is psychological. There is a sense of relief and happiness to be told you are normal, particularly when the examination is thorough. Also there are clear medical advantages. Most illnesses show symptoms before it is too late, and tests can indicate the early stages of heart disease.

A blood pressure reading. Symptoms are often absent with high blood pressure, even when it is severe. Many people complain of headaches or fatigue but as these are so common people often miss them. However high blood pressure is a major risk factor and should be treated by highly effective drugs.

Urine screening for sugar. This simple test can reveal hitherto unsuspected diabetes, which in its early stages may have few symptoms other than lethargy.

Fasting blood fats. This blood test measures the level of cholesterol and triglycerides in your blood. It can be an important indicator of the likelihood of developing a heart attack. The annual medical is therefore helpful. It is not a guarantee that you will live until the next one. Bernard had a totally normal electrocardiogram and had a heart attack a few months later. It could have happened a day later. The ECG shows what is happening to the heart at the same time as the test. It will show abnormalities after an attack but it is not capable of long-term prediction.

Nowadays the number of people having annual medicals is growing and it will become an important factor in our fight against escalating heart disease. But a word of warning. If you are found to be healthy at the annual medical, you might ignore symptoms which develop subsequently. The answer for everyone and particularly people at risk like Bernard is to TAKE NOTE OF SYMPTOMS and DO SOMETHING about them. These symptoms, particularly relating to the heart, are of considerable importance and it is vital to establish what they are.

Chest pain

All of us will have some chest pain of one sort or another in our lives, usually due to muscular strain. The chest is full of muscles which pull the ribs up and down to enable us to breathe. If damaged they cannot be completely rested because you cannot stop breathing, and muscular chest pains tend to linger for quite some time. In addition, the subconscious fear of many men in particular that this is heart pain perpetuates the problem, often for months.

Pains are usually localised in one area, often on the left side. They come and go 'out of the blue'. The pains are often worse in times of stress but tend to occur in the evening or at weekends rather than during the hurly-burly of the day. In extreme cases they are accompanied by a feeling of depression and an awareness of the heart thumping. This is a common condition nowadays but in the past it seemed to manifest itself particularly in times of war. It was first described by a surgeon called Da Costa working in the American Civil War and has become known as 'Da Costa's Syndrome' (syndrome = a collection of signs and symptoms). Many young men who did not want to go to fight developed these left-sided chest pains and thought (and hoped) that they had heart disease so they would not be conscripted. Similar circumstances occurred in the First World War. 'The Soldier's Heart' it was called, and in the Second World War it was given the name, 'The Effort Syndrome'. Although it lacks a suitable name in peacetime it is probably equally common.

This type of localised pain is common. If you can point to the pain with one finger it is almost always musculo-skeletal and not a symptom of a heart attack.

Many medical problems can cause more generalised pain. Organs within the body are not so richly supplied with pain fibres as the skin which, being a defensive shield, is heavily innervated. If a person places a hand on your abdomen and squeezes your stomach you would feel pain and discomfort generally throughout your whole chest and abdomen.

Organs therefore which can produce chest pain are:

The heart
The lungs
The spine
The ribs
The stomach
The duodenum (the tube leading from the stomach)
The gall bladder
The oesophagus (the tube leading to the stomach)

Therefore if you develop pains in your chest they do not necessarily come from your heart. So *do not panic*. A collapsed lung, which is rarely serious, acid regurgitating into the gullet, a stomach ulcer, a duodenal ulcer, gall stones, an infection of the gall bladder and injury to the spine can all mimic exactly pain from the heart. And in Bernard's case it is ironic that while his heart was under severe pressure he was also suffering from a hiatus hernia. The symptoms can be identical.

So the lesson is that if you have any pain in your chest then consult your doctor immediately. The GP will not accuse you of wasting his or her time. Medicine is far from an exact science and much of a doctor's time is spent reassuring people. Because we all

know someone who has suffered a heart attack we have become
slightly neurotic about chest pains. If you have a chest pain, go and
get it checked. Your GP will not mind in the least and all doctors
will prefer to tell you that you are fine rather than anything else.

Breathlessness

If the heart is under strain the lungs become slightly congested
and that makes you feel breathless. We have all experienced
the sensation of breathlessness and although it is not painful
it is uncomfortable and if persistent can be extremely distress-
ing. It is difficult to say when breathlessness is unnatural. We
will all experience breathlessness if we run.

*If you have to stop on a flight of stairs to catch your breath that
is definitely abnormal.* Nevertheless, the commonest cause of
breathlessness is some abnormality of the lungs rather than the
heart. Diseases such as bronchitis, asthma, pneumonia and
pneumoconiosis (a disease common among coal-miners) all
prevent adequate amounts of oxygen reaching the bloodstream
and can create serious breathlessness.

In this country the commonest single cause of breathlessness
is chronic bronchitis known as 'The English disease'. The cold
damp weather often combined with smoking irritates the lining
of the lungs to produce a lot of mucus. This prevents air getting
into the bloodstream as effectively as it should, so creating
breathlessness. The mucus irritates the cough reflex and coughing up phlegm, particularly in the mornings, is the hallmark
of bronchitis. Heart disease rarely presents with a cough and
when it does it is 'dry'. There is no mucus.

People who have anaemia can also be breathless. So just
because you are breathless does not necessarily mean you have
heart trouble. But it is worth a trip to the doctor. The worst
that could happen to you is being sent for a chest X-ray.

Palpitations

Palpitations mean that you are suddenly aware of your heart
beating. Under normal circumstances we are not aware of our
heart at all. If you get a fright you will feel your heart thudding
and that is a form of palpitation. By no means all palpitations

are serious. Most of us will have experienced what we call 'a missed beat' which can be very frightening indeed, but it is very much part of ageing and pretty well everyone will have noticed such an event by the age of 50.

The descriptions of palpitations vary enormously from fluttering to a heavy thumping, and during an 'attack' patients' symptoms may be non-existent, or quite severe chest pain, breathlessness and fainting may occur. Do not be alarmed by palpitations, which are rarely a sign of an impending heart attack. But go and see your doctor. He may be unable to tell you exactly what they are, but he can do an electrocardiogram and decide if your heart is normal.

Electrocardiogram

As we have mentioned the ECG quite a lot throughout this book it is worthwhile looking at what happens. There is certainly no cause to be alarmed and it is totally painless. You are 'wired up' to a small electrical recorder which records the electrical activity coming from your heart. The waveform which is produced indicates the state of your heart.

A wet pad is attached to both arms and legs and a suction pad to the front of your chest. This enables the heart to be 'looked at' in a variety of different directions. It is a completely painless test even if first time you have it you feel you are being put in the electric chair.

The ECG recording will show the rhythmic contraction and relaxation of the heart muscle. When each beat is identical, it is called *sinus rhythm*. Any rhythm which is not like this is an *arrhythmia*. A typical example of this is when the patient experiences what he calls a missed beat. People often think their heart has stopped and it is then followed by a heavy thump. It can be very frightening. But it is in fact by far the commonest type of palpitation and is, to a very large extent, benign (i.e., does not represent heart disease). It often occurs when you are quiet, particularly in bed, and is less likely to happen if you reduce or stop your intake of alcohol and coffee, and smoking.

Similar palpitations are produced by stress. This has the effect of stimulating the body to produce adrenalin, the 'fight or fright' hormone. If you are about to be attacked by a person holding a knife, adrenalin will be rapidly produced and

circulate in the bloodstream. Adrenalin puts the muscles on
edge and at the ready so that you can run away or fight danger
as best you can. As the heart is mostly a special type of muscle,
it too is on edge. The effect of prolonged stress is frequently
to produce extra beats which disappear if your heart rate
increases. As you rush about all day or shout at people your
heart rate stays at about 100 beats per minute at most. When
you relax in bed at night your heart rate comes down to about
60 beats per minute and these extra beats can nip in and give
you a feeling of impending doom.

*Fortunately this form of palpitation is benign and stress alone
will not lead to a heart attack.*

Fatigue

It is very difficult to decide if you have undue tiredness and
very difficult to assess its cause. Almost every disease in the
medical textbook can produce fatigue including depression; on
the other hand, fatigue can herald a heart attack. With a
symptom like this you have to look back six or twelve months
and remember how you were then. If in comparison you are
now going to bed earlier, reluctant to have a social life and
look forward to the weekend as an oasis in the desert, then it's
worth having yourself checked.

Fatigue due to heart disease is physical. You tend to sleep
longer and very soundly and benefit from a sit down at any
time. Many people come home from work having dashed
around all day, have an alcoholic drink or a large meal or both,
sit down in the armchair in front of the fire and fall asleep for
a half to one hour. That is quite normal despite what your
spouse says, although it is rather unsociable.

*Fatigue from the heart is when you spend all your spare time
getting your energy back just to lead a normal active life. That
needs medical assessment.*

Lightheadedness

Dizziness, a sense of the world whirling around, is usually a
symptom of disease of the inner ear, whereas lightheadedness
is a sense of being about to pass out. Lightheadedness is

common in fatigue, depression and a lot of virus infections so does not automatically mean that disaster is round the corner.

If the heart slows dramatically or speeds up excessively the amount of blood being pumped to the brain is reduced and a feeling of faintness may occur. Even when the cause of the symptoms is directly due to the heart it may not be serious. Many young people develop sudden fast heart rates and feel quite unwell but they do not have any underlying heart disease.

Ankle-swelling

It would be very hard indeed for ankle-swelling to present as the first sign of heart disease. It is normally quite a late sign and would be preceded by such symptoms as breathlessness and fatigue. Ankle-swelling is generally caused by the body retaining fluid and, because of the effects of gravity, it retains it in its lowest part, i.e., ankles and feet. It is ankle-swelling rather than foot-swelling, because we wear shoes.

When we lie in bed the fluid drains to the middle of the back because that is then the lowest part of the body. Thus when we wake up the fluid has magically disappeared from the ankles but re-accumulates during the day. The commonest cause of ankle-swelling is varicose veins. Usually one side is worse than the other.

Equally common is the ankle-swelling associated with sitting in an aircraft for long spells. With the legs often immobile in a tight space blood does not flow back to the heart very well and fluid seeps out into the ankles.

Any situation where one ankle is more swollen than the other is likely to be something other than heart disease. *In heart disease ankle-swelling occurs in both ankles.*

So overall, it is possible to identify symptoms of a heart attack in advance. A chest pain is the obvious sign but is not inevitably from the heart. But you know your own risk factors better than anyone and, if experiencing any of the symptoms I have described, then see a doctor immediately.

7. The big day

BERNARD FALK

I left hospital in a jubilant mood and did a little hop, skip and jump on the way. Not many people think that a hiatus hernia is worth celebrating but then it clearly wasn't my heart that was causing the pain. The doctors had diagnosed that there was something wrong with my digestive system, so what? After years of abusing my health I had got away with it. I was delighted to have a pain in the gut instead of a problem with the heart.

Dr Blackwood has said that it is often hard to differentiate between a heart attack and many other illnesses which can show the same symptoms. Apart from that the pain in my chest had been on holiday for a couple of days and if I had to moderate my eating habits to cope with a hiatus hernia then so be it. As I headed resolutely towards my favourite bar life looked pretty good.

Strange to think that I would end up in a special care unit that evening suffering from a heart attack.

Whisky has been my favourite tipple for many a year. I love the taste of the stuff. One Scotch, preferably a good earthy malt, normally whets the appetite for another Scotch and so on. My capacity is such that I can down three or four large ones and still work in the afternoon. On Friday 30th May I had six or seven large ones and decided that the work could get stuffed. I accompanied this modest celebration by munching my way through a 10 oz. sirloin steak and a baked potato. Clearly the hiatus hernia would have to wait for a day or two as well.

The long-suffering people with whom I work are fairly used to the sight of their beloved chairman and leader weaving his way unsteadily towards the executive office. After I've been having a celebration lunch they take bets on whether I will make it to the office intact or walk through a glass door without opening it.

This time I gritted my teeth and managed to reach my chair without any loss of dignity. Everyone was delighted that the pain I had been suffering in the chest for a couple of weeks was a digestive problem and not the heart. Indeed we decided to open a bottle of champagne (or two) to continue the celebration. Only amateurs mix their drinks. Being a professional I stuck to Scotch.

Then, after proving my new-found fitness by demonstrating the proper way to do a tango across a table-top, I shooed everyone out of the office and settled down to write my radio script for 'Breakaway'. It normally has to be finished on a Friday night ready for the live show the following morning.

I typed the first page. And the pain came. I gasped. Surely it couldn't be back? It was back all right and with such a vengeance that it seemed to be making up for its absence over the previous few days. It struck deep into the left side of my chest as before, shot down the left arm into the fingers. The sharp stabbing sensation in the chest and the throbbing ache as an afterburn almost paralysed one side of my body. God! It had never been quite as bad as this. I cursed the Scotch. I damned my steak lunch to hell. I stood up to ease the pain. This had always worked before. This time the bastard retaliated by slamming across the front of my chest. I doubled up and it slewed off the shoulder back down the arm. For the first time I felt the tingling in the tips of my fingers on the left hand.

For the first time I felt fear.

'It can't be a heart attack,' I said to myself. 'I've been checked out. I'm in the clear. It's this blasted hiatus hernia. I ate and drank too much for lunch. I might be a bit of an old pisshead and serves me right but I never imagined I would pay for lunch like this.'

A worried colleague, seeing me doubled up across my desk, poked her head around the corner of the office and asked if I was all right. It was a strange sensation. I felt more embarrassed than anything. I had never experienced real pain before, nothing like this. In a way I felt better by locking myself away. I suppose I was terrified in case I started crying and lost control.

I looked at my watch. 'Christ, it's been going on now for

twenty minutes. That's longer than normal.' I stumbled into
the gents and locked the door. I stood leaning against the wall
staring down at the bowl. It's amazing what you think of. Like
getting the place painted or buying a new towel. Occasionally
my workmates would hammer on the door and ask if I needed
help. I told them to stay away.

'It's going,' I thought. It wasn't. My body was getting used
to it or else I was getting weaker. I tried to light a cigarette
but dropped the matches and the pain leapt back pushing my
backbone rigid before shooting its journey down the arm
to the fingers. Somehow, walking slowly with my left hand
dangling rather uselessly, I made it back to my office. I had
been in there for over an hour. And it would not go away, two
hours, three. It would not go away.

I tried to think . . . there is a woman in front of me, a
colleague and friend for many years. I don't care about dignity.
I need help, anything.

I found myself crying on her shoulder. There was no shame.
The pain rested, the sharpness reduced to an ache. It kicked
again. I was on my knees and crying. There was nothing other
than pain.

For whatever ludicrous reason I was determined to make it
home. Criminal folly perhaps when you consider I was having
a gold-carat heart attack.

But I got it into my mind that if I made it home through
the Friday night rush-hour traffic then it might prove there
was nothing very much wrong with me. I reached the car and
drove, slowly, foolishly. I had been on the phone warning my
wife, Linda. She offered to come the twenty-five miles into
London to fetch me but Linda was six months pregnant and
I insisted on making it home myself.

I cannot remember very much about that journey. The pain
was there, flowing like an ebb tide, hot and cold in intensity,
as I slowly made it home. I asked for the doctor as Linda
half-carried me through the door.

'I told him you were in great pain but he wondered if
you could make it round to the surgery,' she said. The
tears of pain turned to seething anger. I grabbed the phone
and rang the doctor. I felt ashamed later for abusing him.
He could not know. He was busy enough with other patients

It's going, I thought. It wasn't.

and anyway within ten minutes he was standing at my bedside.

He listened patiently and caringly as I stumbled out the story. The pain, the hospital in the morning, the diagnosis that I had a hiatus hernia. As I lay propped up on the bed, he felt my pulse and took my blood pressure. One was racing. The other was through the roof. I remember him on the phone. 'Roger, could you come,' I heard him say.

And so a man called Roger Blackwood entered my life: cardiologist. 'Good God, it might be my heart,' I thought. He fastened rubber suckers to my chest. They were attached to a strange-looking object which he carried in a briefcase, his portable ECG.

'I think you ought to be in hospital, old chap,' I heard him say. 'I would like you to go now. It is better we crack this thing for good. Maybe it is the hernia, perhaps you could have a spot of trouble with your pancreas but I would like you in tonight and I'll come and see you later.'

Linda helped me to pack a suitcase and she drove me to the Nuffield Hospital in Slough. I was worried about her condition and insisted that I carried my suitcase and a heavy briefcase into the hospital and up to the ward.

There people strapped wires and tubes to my body. There were needles in the left side, rubber things on my chest and machines all over the place, odd contraptions that went blip, blip, blip.

'Funny thing for someone with a wonky digestion,' I thought. They took blood, put another injection in my arm, this time for the pain. I felt sleepy and, what a bloody miracle, the pain began to go away, reducing to a dull ache in the left side of my chest. I saw Roger Blackwood standing beside the bed.

'I think you ought to prepare yourself for the chance that it's not a digestive problem, old chap,' he said. 'We will tell from the blood test what has gone wrong.

'But I think you've had a heart attack.'

DR ROGER BLACKWOOD

Much of medicine is far from being understood. The reality is that we do not know what actually precipitates a heart attack.

Indeed the event can show itself in so many ways that it can be missed completely by both doctor and patient.

The classical presentation is difficult to miss. The patient experiences severe chest pain, sometimes so severe that he thinks he is about to die. In addition he may look pale, be breathless, feel lightheaded and be aware of his heart beating. At the other end of the scale a heart attack can be completely symptomless. The patient may just feel a bit 'off-colour' for a day or two.

A heart attack is the blockage of an artery in the heart. When the blood supply to any part of the heart is stopped abruptly, that part gradually dies off, in a matter of two to three hours. During this phase the chest pain is intense. An area around this dead zone will be partly damaged but not die because it can get a small supply of blood from another blood vessel.

This damaged area partially dies while the rest may return to normal. This whole process of a heart attack takes place over about twenty-four hours.

Whatever we do, the area immediately around the blocked artery will die, but the partly injured area is best managed by making the heart do the least possible work. Clearly bed rest is the immediate answer, which is why the majority of patients in the first stages of a heart attack are admitted to hospital.

However, many people may be able to rest at home just as well as in hospital. If your own doctor is prepared to look after you there may be some merits in recovering at home. It is the balance between the friendly environment of home, but without immediate medical attention and high technical equipment, or, on the other hand, the rather alien and sometimes frightening environment of a hospital ward but which has all modern resuscitation facilities.

If you are in a situation where you are with someone who you think is having a heart attack, you should call a doctor immediately. If for any reason you cannot contact your doctor, then dial 999 without hesitation. The ambulance services are very well aware of the possible problems of a coronary and will be there very rapidly indeed.

In the meantime the essence of treatment is to stay calm. Talk quietly and in a matter-of-fact way to the patient. If you get frightened and show it, the patient will be more worried and will produce even more adrenalin in his or her body. This makes the heart work faster and tends to make the heart attack worse. Until a medical team arrives there is nothing practical you can do except stay with the person concerned and chatter away.

When the doctor arrives he will first try to confirm whether the person has had a heart attack. He may be able to do this in a matter of seconds, or he may need to ask questions for quite some time. If the pain is severe he will not hesitate to give an injection of morphine or one its analogues or give a tablet under the tongue which is rapidly absorbed. Morphine is used because it is excellent at taking away the pain, because it makes the patient feel cheerful and relaxed, and because it helps the heart to do less work.

The doctor will then decide whether to admit the patient to hospital or to keep him at home. If he is going to admit him he will normally summon an ambulance and stay with him until it arrives. If the doctor keeps the patient at home he may take a heart tracing on an ECG machine and then take a sample of blood.

When I arrived at Bernard's house that night there were a lot of questions to ask because his history was not really classical of a coronary and he already had a diagnosis of hiatus hernia. He was intensely irritated by his pain and very frightened.

We went over the pain's relationship to his eating, his Civil Aviation medical, which is very exacting, his first flight and his barium meal. Only glimpses of his history suggested its cardiac origin, but after doing an ECG it was all too obvious. He put up less fight than I expected about going to hospital, probably because deep down he knew what it was. I said to him that I thought it might be his pancreas because I did not want to frighten him at that point, after all he had been through. A sudden shock on top of all that pain might have finished him off. He was cross enough as it was.

If I had called an ambulance he would have questioned what was going on and been even more frightened. After all he was still walking around the room and his wife had already volunteered to drive him to the hospital which was only ten minutes away. It seemed sensible to get on with it that way. The ECG showed only a very small heart attack so I did not feel there was much danger. I wanted Bernard in hospital so that we could do all the confirmatory tests on his heart to prove the exact nature of what he had as well as give him something for his pain.

Once in hospital he was much calmer and after an intravenous dose of morphine became thoroughly relaxed. He needed some tablets for his blood pressure and after all this was done I told him he had had a small heart attack and likened it to breaking a leg. Once you are in control of the situation, the sooner you tell the patient the better.

Now, months later, Bernard complains that he received no treatment apart from an injection to ease the pain. But there is no actual treatment of the heart attack itself. At present there is no way we can actually nip in and remove the clot to reverse the heart attack. An operation to remove the clot carries about the same risk of death as a heart attack itself and with all the traumas that it entails it is not really worth considering.

There are over 200,000 heart attacks a year in this country. If we tried to operate on them all this would put an impossible burden on the National Health Service. In practice one would have to operate almost immediately after a heart attack so the practicalities become ridiculous. In the next few years a new substance called 'tissue plasmin activator' may become available, which, in a fairly high proportion of patients, will dissolve the clot. This will be a major breakthrough and is just one example of the way medical science is advancing on heart disease. It will never be totally eradicated in human beings but it is safe to say that as the era of artificial hearts moves nearer, the longer you live and take care of yourself the more medical science catches up. When Bernard's father died thirty years ago by-pass surgery to replace damaged or blocked arteries was hardly thought of, transplants were just a figment in a science fiction writer's imagination and the drugs available to doctors were very limited. Bernard's father probably had exceptionally high blood pressure but in those days there were no such things as Beta-Blockers which his son now takes each day to spare his heart excessive strain.

So if we cannot dissolve the clot and take away the heart attack, why do we admit the patient to hospital at all? The answer is that we can treat the complications which result from

a heart attack, some of which are quite deadly. The majority
of these occur in the first forty-eight hours, and so careful
monitoring during this period is of enormous value. That's
why two highly trained and dedicated nurses watched Bernard
day and night for the first two days in hospital. In the days
before coronary care units the number of people who died
from a heart attack was about 35 per cent. Now it is between
10 and 15 per cent. This may sound high but the statistics
include patients up to the age of 100. In fact the percentage of
younger people is very much lower than the overall figure.

Also it is not possible to know which patient is going to
develop complications. The majority do not, but in those who
do the chief problem is that of a cardiac arrest. This literally
means what it says. The heart stops beating. In these early
stages it is due to what can be best described as a kind of
'electrical fault' and if corrected quickly the heart will escape
comparatively unscathed. This coined the rather nauseating
phrase—'the heart too young to die'. The heart is an electrical
pump. Electricity flows down the heart and is immediately
followed by contraction. The flow of electricity has to be in an
orderly fashion so that contraction is co-ordinated.

The commonest cause of cardiac arrest is something called
'ventricular fibrillation'. In this the electrical activity is chaotic
so that there is no contraction of the heart at all. The heart
quivers and is described as being like a bag of worms. No
blood is pumped out of the heart and in particular no blood
reaches the brain. Starved of oxygen and sugar the brain cells
begin to die within three minutes of the heart stopping. The
patient will be unconscious and unless his heart is started very
quickly brain-death will occur. Even if the heart starts later
the patient may never wake up again. This is why there is such
urgency when a cardiac arrest occurs. In hospital doctors will
run to the patient as fast as they can and such a situation is
clearly not possible to deal with in the home. This is one of
the main reasons for admitting someone to hospital where—
should an arrest occur—at least he has a chance. So while
Bernard may wonder why he had to go to hospital just to
receive one injection the real reason was to avoid any further
risk.

Of those who are going to die after a heart attack 30–50 per cent do so within the first hour and the majority of these have ventricular fibrillation. If you develop ventricular fibrillation it is very simple to deal with as long as action is taken quickly. All you need to do is send an electric shock to the heart which wipes out all the quivering electrical charges and allows normal rhythm to start again. Two paddles are placed on the chest and the button pressed. A shock of 400 joules (a bit like touching the mains for one to two seconds) blasts into the heart. After a delay of one or two seconds the heart will probably start beating again. Shocking the patient is very commonly performed at a cardiac arrest and is so simple it can be done by doctors, nurses and ambulance men with relatively little training. It is quite painless for the patient since he is unconscious at the time.

This routine technique can save many lives but the difficulty has been that most deaths occur so early after a heart attack that it is before the patient has reached hospital. The equipment simply isn't there when you most need it. However, coronary care ambulances have been introduced to solve this problem. In the ambulance all the equipment required to resuscitate the patient is installed and is transferred rapidly to the suspected heart attack. If the patient should then have a cardiac arrest the ambulance men can deliver the shock immediately. The first coronary care ambulance in this country started in Belfast and it is now acknowledged that about 5 per cent of patients picked up by the teams have a cardiac arrest and survive. Translated into the whole country this could be as many as 10,000 people a year who would otherwise have died.

From a patient's point of view the problem is pain. Once that is dulled he will feel so thankful that he will not realise the full significance of what has happened. This will not dawn upon him for a day or two. Those relatives close to the patient will be far more concerned, but as long as they are informed about what is going on most cope remarkably well. As for the doctor, well he does very little actual treatment of the heart attack but he does act as a symbol of reassurance and security to the patient and relatives. Medicine is much more of an art than a science.

In Bernard's case he was sitting up in bed and having to be restrained from walking to the lavatory only twenty-four hours after his heart attack. His blood tests confirmed that he had suffered a myocardial infarction, a blood clot in an artery in the heart, so the next challenge was to keep the blighter alive. That meant persuading him to change his lifestyle. We call it 'rehabilitation' and in the care of coronary patients and the overall fight against heart disease it is one of the most important factors of all.

8. A broken heart

BERNARD FALK

Survival is a very basic human instinct. It dominates everything and controls emotions like fear. It is just as well. Fear keeps us alive. After a heart attack you are very frightened indeed. That's how I felt before an injection of morphine sent me quickly into a restless sleep. I was in the coronary care unit of the hospital. I knew it was my heart, that the pain was coming from the very object which pumps the blood around my body. This was very bad news indeed. For the first time it occurred to me that there was a possibility I might die. This was even worse news. But then I thought: To hell with it. The thing I can hear thumping away with fright sounds distinctly like my heart. Either that or the 'thump, thump, thump' noise is the sound of my knees knocking.

From that moment on, even as I dozed, I became determined to survive and even then I was conscious of the fact that this would mean a dramatic change in the way I looked after myself, that life as I had known it would never be the same again.

That night in the coronary care unit Mark and Mary entered my life, or at least they were responsible, along with my ticker, for ensuring it continued. I wonder how many people like me have wanted to tell Enoch Powell that I'm glad we didn't 'send them home'? If we had, then a lot of white folks would have been in the happy hunting grounds before their time. Mark and Mary were both first-generation immigrants from the West Indies, and they are skilled, caring, professional 'angels' who on one night in May helped ensure that a very frightened overweight Liverpudlian didn't become an angel himself.

Mark and Mary are experienced in the care of cardiac patients. They sat side by side throughout the night just watching me, their eyes never off the snoozing patient nor the machines monitoring the activity of my heart. I slept in fits and bursts. Occasionally I glanced at the equipment beside my bed and couldn't resist whispering, 'Keep ticking you sod,' as the wavy electronic lines showed what was happening inside.

Every half an hour or so I was conscious of gentle but firm hands on my body and arms as they took my pulse and blood pressure. Although I could not see it another machine called a defibrillator stood waiting. It would pass an electric shock into my heart if I suffered a cardiac arrest.

In my left arm Mary had inserted a tube into the main vein. At the time it just seemed like another bit of wiring coming out of my body. In fact this tube, which was flushed out with water at regular intervals, would be used to pump drugs straight into the system in an emergency. Now and again I was given another ECG. It all seemed like a right palaver but strangely in retrospect you tend to remember the little things.

Each time I crossed my ankles to get more comfortable one of my angels would give me a sharp tap on the leg and make me uncross them. It became quite irritating but apparently this can block off part of your circulation and that's the last thing you need with a heart attack.

I shall never forget Mark and Mary, not only for their medical skill—you could guarantee that from all the nurses—but for the reassurance they gave me during a very stressful few hours of my life. When you are frightened and in pain there's nothing like the warmth of another human being. In between the brief periods of sleep Mark told me about his home in the West Indies. We chatted about England's chances of winning the test matches during the forthcoming cricket season (enough to give any patriotic cricket lover another heart attack). It was the small talk, the trivialities of life, that helped take my mind off the enormity of my problems and I was grateful for a chance to discuss Ian Botham's drug offences, why Viv Richards was the world's greatest batsman and so on. It helped me to reach the dawn. I watched the sunlight of a spring morning filtering through the curtains and felt in a very good frame of mind to face the traumas of the day.

The first thing I noticed was that the pain had gone. The damned thing had disappeared, vanished. Perhaps it had never happened. Maybe I imagined the whole thing. The doctors had got it wrong. Was Roger an idiot too? Clearly they had made a serious mistake in their diagnosis. The blood tests would show that I really had a spot of heart burn. I would be home for lunch, hardly the worse for wear.

What folly, I thought to myself, reaching for a cigarette, that I should end up here, with all these sick people. Such madness that someone like me could actually have trouble with his heart. I looked for a telephone to call my office with the idea of holding a forthcoming board meeting in the hospital if they wouldn't let me out.

Perhaps I could persuade my wife to bring in a bottle of Scotch? I schemed. And how about a real humdinger of a party to welcome me home? What a rave up that would be. Lots of food and boy would I drink myself silly. . . .

Roger Blackwood, the cardiologist, was standing at the foot of the bed. He didn't mess about and while he spoke the world stood upside down.

'We have the results of the blood test,' he said gently. 'It was a mild heart attack, and please believe me, you are going to be all right. It's a bit like a broken leg. It will heal. You now have a chance. You have a chance to change your lifestyle. You have been lucky. You have been given a warning. And from now on whether you live to be a ripe old age is largely up to you.'

'Fuck,' I said. No one winced. Clearly the nurses standing with Roger had heard it all before. 'But the pain has gone,' I said. 'I feel great, wonderful, surely there's some mistake?' Believe me it's only later you feel a fool, not when you're jabbering away squeezing your pyjama trousers and clutching at straws.

Roger is a kindly man. He probably deals with blithering idiots like this every day of his life. It amazes me he doesn't suffer from stress himself. It would drive me round the twist, coping with the extremes of the human condition. As part of his normal work, that could mean sudden death, a crippled body, a career over, a job gone, the pain, distress and the fear.

Patiently that morning he explained that a small part of my heart muscle had been damaged. There had been a blockage of an artery. This had caused a scar, so small perhaps that you could not see it with the naked eye. The pain had gone because the bit of heart muscle affected had died. What I had to do now was rest and recover. Then we could find out what caused the blockage in the first place and by moderate changes in my lifestyle I could live to a good old age.

Then he was gone, leaving me to digest the enormity of what I had heard. This had to wait a while for breakfast. It's amazing how a boiled egg, toast and tea can divert you away from the effort of feeling sorry for yourself. I thought of crying but then bits of yolk could have dribbled off the shaking spoon on to my chest. Everyone knows that there's nothing worse than congealed yolk on your chest. I abandoned the thought of sobbing and ate my egg instead.

I thought over what Roger had said. So there was no doubt then. Blast! How would Linda take it? What would happen to my job, my company? I imagined the bailiffs tramping across the roses, loading the furniture into a huge van while my frantic wife and weeping children begged in the streets for bread.

Then I clung to the reassuring things he had said. Roger has a great ability to convince patients that they have not reached the end of the line. You might be playing football when someone hacks off two arms and both legs. If Roger was the team manager he would say, 'Bang the ball in with your head.' He realised that in the early stages of rehabilitation the cardiac patient has mental worries to overcome. The body will heal but in the meantime you could worry yourself to death.

That morning as I contemplated my fate there was one blessed relief. The pain had gone. I know I've mentioned that before but to me it really mattered. In fact apart from an odd twinge the pain has never returned.

One of the few good things about being a cardiac patient is that you can suffer a heart attack and if there is no serious damage or major blockage of the arteries you can feel on top of the world a few days later. The pain is severe while it lasts but then you rapidly return to normal. In my case I did not feel sick, not physically. The psychological problems were another matter. Sorting out the old brain-box, getting your mind right, that's the worst hurdle. Lying in the coronary care unit I felt grateful to be alive. But I realised for the first time in my life that I was just a vulnerable twit the same as anyone

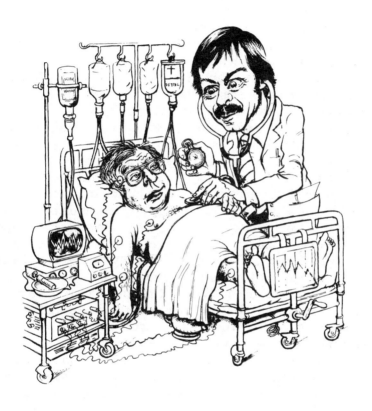

I became determined to survive

else. It had happened to me, not the other chap, but me. One
of the first basic emotions I felt was anger, against myself, that
I had spent so many years punishing my body, ignoring my
health, and now, just like anyone else, I was having to pay the
price.

Fortunately hospital is a great leveller and the day-to-day
routine brings you sharply back to earth. The other nurses of
the coronary care unit arrived and relieved Mark and Mary's
night shift. There was Paul, an exotic character from Manchester, a brilliant professional chargehand nurse with a heart of
gold and an accent straight out of Coronation Street. The girls,
Gloria, Jill, Eva, a bevy of beauties who would rapidly become
good friends. Soon I was feeling a lot better, apart from a
growing sensation that I had a pain in my bum.

Remember that on the day of my heart attack I had been to
the hospital for a barium meal. This meant swallowing a
pinkish substance which showed up on a television monitor as
it progressed down the digestive system. However that liquid
soon turns to concrete and what goes in must come out, if you
see what I mean. The morning after my heart attack I was
desperate and Paul was furious at my refusal to use a bed-pan.
'Sit on that,' he yelled. 'Won't,' I replied. On such are great
friendships forged. But you know how trivialities can be elevated out of all proportion. I was determined to get out of bed
and make it to the lavatory on my own. Perhaps I was trying
to prove to myself that I wasn't a bed-ridden invalid or maybe
I was suffering from premature senility. Either way I would
heartily like to thank all those doctors who recommended that
I should swallow a pint of concrete just a few hours before my
heart attack. The strain of passing the concrete through the
system nearly gave me another.

Then, bless them, the visitors began to arrive. My wife, my
ex-wife and three of my five children, a couple of close friends
and colleagues from work. The Lucozade-and-grapes brigade.
You are glad to see them and pleased that everyone says you
are looking well. They could hardly say that you were looking
lousy could they? Still you never know. My mother's age
prevented her from joining the happy throng. Instead she had
been on the phone to remind my wife that when I lived 'at
home' twenty-five years earlier I had had no trouble with heart

attacks and the like. Clearly my wife's cooking had brought it on.

Thankfully my loved ones realised that a ten-to-fifteen minute visit is wonderful. Longer and it tires the patient. So they ate the grapes and went.

As for me, well, soon I settled into a daily routine. I remained for two days in the coronary care unit before being unplugged from the various machines and placed in a room on my own. In a National Health Hospital patients mix together in the medical wards and get great benefit in sharing companionship with heart sufferers like themselves. It offers great consolation. You realise how many are in the same boat as you and that some are considerably worse. But in the immediate aftermath of my heart attack I was grateful that I could afford the cost of a room on my own. I had to pawn the family silver and put the goldfish on emergency rations but I thought it was worth it at the time.

I was also glad to learn that heart patients are encouraged to eat three square meals a day. Mind you I did notice that the portions served up were smaller than I was used to and that most of the dishes contained less fatty foods. One day I ordered fish and chips for a treat. The fish was grilled, without batter around it, a sort of naked white splodge (ghastly), and I received no less than FIVE chips as a ration. All clever stuff this. You begin to realise that you can eat more in quantity if you have salad, vegetables and fruit instead.

Of course alcohol was banned. Quickly I made emergency plans to confuse the issue. A half-bottle of Scotch smuggled in by Ken, an understanding friend (and a bum as well) was quickly dispensed into a Lucozade bottle. I am sure the world has been waiting to learn that Scotch and Lucozade look remarkably similar. Mind you it didn't fool them for long. Then I found a miracle in the drawer. A half-smoked cigarette. Eagerly I grabbed the stub and lit it. An even greater miracle. I coughed, hating the thing. I resolved to keep the dog-end for an emergency just in case I couldn't stand total abstinence from cigarettes and started banging my head on the wall. But I said to myself: 'These things will kill you if you don't leave them alone.' It was the start of a serious attempt to break the habit for good.

Surprisingly the atmosphere in a coronary care unit is normally cheerful, except when someone dies, which tends to put a bit of a damper on things. I have explained that some patients feel quite normal, free of pain, and those are often people who have suffered a major heart attack, even a cardiac arrest, a few days before. It helps that a lot of the people you meet in hospital are like you—knackered because of the way they have lived. In Slough and later at the National Heart Hospital in London there was lots of communal remorse. Again like me, I heard many good resolutions being made. Isn't it sad that in spite of all our excellent intentions a high percentage of cardiac patients have a secondary attack largely as a direct result of refusing to change their lifestyle?

Lying in hospital wired up to machines and feeling extremely sorry for yourself it is easy to say, 'I will lose weight, take exercise, give up smoking, cut down on my workload, reduce the amount of stress.' And so we do for a few weeks during the early stages of rehabilitation. But then a majority, a foolish majority, stray back to their bad old ways and end up in coronary care once more. Quite a number end up in coffins too.

As for me, well, I remained in hospital for a week. Then my wife arrived to take me home. Ahead lay six weeks of rest and rehabilitation. The first stage of recovery was over. But what lay in store was perhaps the greatest trial of all. Being at home can be hell not only for the cardiac patient but for his family too.

DR ROGER BLACKWOOD

What went wrong?

Bernard was lucky he ended up in a hospital's special care unit. The advance of specialised coronary care units has been a major breakthrough in the treatment of cardiac patients and I want to devote a little time explaining their value. To do this we must look at the way we treated heart patients in the past.

First, let's look at the working of the heart itself. It will help us to understand what went wrong with Bernard's. The heart is a piece of muscle, shaped like the cup of your hand. When

Bernard is resting, and that's not very often, his heart should pump about five litres of blood around his corporate frame each minute. When walking, and in his case that's not very often either, then his heart should pump about ten litres of blood a minute, rising on some occasions up to thirty litres a minute. In an average lifetime Bernard's heart will pump enough blood to fill the Albert Hall (providing he lasts that long by taking better care of himself). As for the heart muscle itself, that's driven by electricity, a contraction, which goes from the top to the bottom of the heart.

There are two sides of the heart, the right and left. If we imagine blood travelling from your finger tips we can follow it round your body. Blood travels back to the heart along veins which run the length of your arm, across your chest and into your heart. This is called the right atrium. Then it passes through a one-way valve into a pumping chamber, called the right ventricle. The right ventricle squeezes, forcing blood into the lungs so that it can pick up oxygen. From the lungs the blood goes into a collecting chamber called the left atrium. The blood then passes through another one-way valve to the main pumping chamber of the heart, which is called the left ventricle. As the left ventricle squeezes, the blood pressure rises, and blood pours out of the heart into the main blood vessels. This is the aorta. It measures about one inch in diameter. This blood vessel leads round the body sending branches to all parts, the head and brain, arms and legs, kidneys and liver and so on.

When Bernard had a heart attack an area of his heart muscle died off. In his case a very small amount was affected. Also only the left ventricle was involved. All the other chambers of a heart manage to work well under low pressure and the changes to the heart during an attack tend to reduce the amount of blood that is being pumped. If this is a significant amount then there can be heart failure and Bernard was lucky that this did not happen to him; lucky too that there was no damage to the electrical system of his heart which then could become either haphazard for a short time or cease altogether.

Coronary Care Unit

At the hospital which admitted Bernard there is a special care unit. It caters for patients with a variety of problems including cardiac cases and is typical of the coronary care units in a large number of NHS hospitals. In a Coronary Care Unit (CCU) the job of the doctors and nurses is to deal with any problems which might arise from either electrical or muscular damage. Nowadays we take CCUs for granted but the first one was only set up in 1962. Bernard had a far better chance of surviving, if things had gone wrong after his heart attack, than his father who died three years before CCUs were introduced. It shows the dramatic development in relatively few years.

Bernard was lucky he did not have his heart attack in the 1950s, when, sadly, treatment then was little more than nursing care. A heart attack was known to take about six weeks to heal so Bernard would have been ordered to remain almost immobile for much of that time—an idea which has now been discarded because it was found to cause further health hazards.

Also in the 1950s a heart attack was thought of as 'serious', and many patients were advised to retire from work immediately. Asking Bernard to retire would be enough to kill him off, but it happened very regularly to perfectly fit people recovering from a heart attack thirty-odd years ago. The entire arrangement was psychologically devastating.

The only treatment in those days was using a method called 'anticoagulation'. This stopped the blood clotting quickly in an attempt to prevent another heart attack. But the results of trials were so disappointing that this method was abandoned.

Bernard was also fortunate that he had the care of doctors and nurses specialising in coronary patients. When his father suffered from heart disease people were rushed into open wards, and many died suddenly and unexpectedly. It was assumed that they died because the muscle had given out which stopped the heart functioning. It was a quite spectacular advance when an enterprising group of doctors from the Hammersmith Hospital in London and Philadelphia in the United States began to look at the electrical aspect of the heart instead of the muscular one.

The ramifications of their work live with us daily and countless millions of heart patients owe their lives to this research.

These American doctors started to record the electrical activity continuously in patients who had suffered heart attacks. This monitoring went on for twenty-four hours and during the recordings several kilometres of paper were required to read the electrical activity in each patient.

What they discovered was quite new. Previously the electrical activity of the heart was thought to be quite irrelevant. However, on observing these patients, the read-outs showed large amounts of electrical abnormalities, some leading to chaotic electrical activity within the heart. These are ventricular fibrillations which can cause cardiac arrest. Clearly a large number of patients died from *electrical* not *muscular* damage. It was a major breakthrough in understanding the cause and subsequent treatment of heart attacks.

Cardiac arrest

I have already described how ventricular fibrillation (the heart quivering like a mass of jelly) can be dealt with by delivering an electrical shock. In 1960 this method was only just being introduced. A scientist had shocked animal hearts into action as long ago as 1933 but it wasn't tried on man until 1947. During this period only operating theatres were equipped to deliver shocks so if you suffered a cardiac arrest you had to be undergoing surgery to stand a chance. In 1956 however a doctor in the United States had a heart attack whilst walking around the ward of a hospital and he went into ventricular fibrillation. He was rushed to the operating theatre and was successfully revived. He suffered only from a minor loss of memory. Soon other cases followed and defibrillators became part of a hospital's standard equipment.

So with much more available in the art of resuscitation the first coronary care units were started in 1962 although one experimental unit had begun in London a few years earlier. They got off to a disastrous start. In the first American unit, doctors got so bored sitting around looking at patients for hours on end waiting for something to happen, that they threatened to strike. Fortunately by the time Bernard became a patient nurses had been trained in resuscitation and are now the backbone of any CCU.

The consequences for patients have been quite profound. From the start of CCUs the hospital death rate halved almost overnight—from 40 to 20 per cent. It is now routine for most heart attack patients to be admitted to a CCU or specific 'monitored area'.

This explains some of the background to the treatment of heart patients but also the equipment which Bernard saw during his first night in the coronary care unit. In fact Bernard suffered a relatively mild attack but it is worth examining what we could have done for him had his condition been a lot worse.

Say that his heart had developed a dangerous rhythm and he had suffered a cardiac arrest. He could have been shocked into a revival using the defibrillator alongside his bed. But what if by some chance the machinery was elsewhere in the hospital, or had broken down, or say there was a major electrical failure in the hospital itself? Then Bernard would have needed all the skill and experience of Mark and Mary, the nurses who sat watching him all night.

In a cardiac arrest Bernard's brain would have begun to die within three minutes. Without a machine Mark and Mary would have given Bernard an external cardiac massage. This is a method of pressing on the chest wall in order to keep blood flowing to the brain during the vital minutes. By pressing the bone at the front of the chest (the sternum) towards the backbone it is possible effectively to 'squash' the heart and force its contents, the blood, around the body. The sort of weight required to press on the chest is about that of the top half of your body. If it is excessive a rib might be broken.

So what could have happened to Bernard? He might have faced two basic problems—electrical or mechanical. I shall deal with the electrical problems first.

Electrical problems

If the electrics go wrong three things can happen:

- The heart stops—that's a cardiac arrest.
- The heart goes too slowly—which is called a bradycardia.
- The heart goes too fast—called a tachycardia.

I have already described the procedure for a cardiac arrest.

If his heart had gone too fast then the nurses would have administered a drug through the tube inserted in Bernard's arm. This drug would have gone directly through the vein to slow his heart. This could have been followed by tablets which do the same thing. A fast heart can be worrying for two reasons. If your heart is beating at a normal rate e.g. 60 beats/min., it has almost one second to fill between each beat. This is more than sufficient time for it to acquire the 70–80 mls of blood from the collecting chamber. If the heart is going at 180 beats/min. there will be scarcely any time for filling and much less blood will be pumped out by the heart in any given time. If the heart produces less and less blood, less and less will circulate to the brain, kidneys and heart, and heart failure will occur. The second problem is that if your heart is beating at 180 beats per minute it is using up a lot of energy and your muscle may weaken as a result. Again heart failure may occur. Not all fast heart rhythms are dangerous and each patient is different, so treatment will vary enormously from patient to patient.

Now what if Bernard's heart had been pumping too slowly? Then he could have suffered heart failure because not enough blood was being pumped out of the heart. At 60 beats/min. the resting cardiac output would be about five litres a minute. At 30 beats/min. this might go down to two and a half litres a minute which would make the patient feel rotten. Drugs can help the situation but not always. You will have heard of the heart pacemaker. It is used in situations like this and is a very simple medical procedure. A thin, flexible plastic wire would have been introduced into a blood vessel in Bernard's neck, by his collar bone and guided into his heart using an X-ray machine. He would have felt no pain.

There are no pain fibres on the inside of the blood vessels in the heart so you cannot feel it once it is inside you. The tip of the wire is placed at the bottom of your heart resting against its inside. Then a tiny electrical current (about 3v), which you cannot feel, passes down the wire and stimulates the heart muscles to contract. The machine attached to the other end of the wire is set at about 70 shocks per minute so that your heart will beat about 70 times per minute.

So as you can see we can control electrical problems fairly well. But what would have happened if Bernard had suffered a *muscular* problem?

Muscular problems

Although dead muscle is dead and therefore can contribute nothing to the pumping action of the heart, the rest of the muscle can also be affected. In a heart attack some muscle may be damaged and therefore not contracting so well. To give this area a bit of a kick, and to make the normal muscle work a bit harder, certain drugs can be administered through the veins to stimulate the heart. If the blood pressure falls, these drugs will raise it back towards normal. Examples of these drugs are Dobutamine, Dopamine and Isoprenaline.

Bernard was lucky in that he did not develop any of these complications. In fact after a heart attack only a relatively small number of patients actually develop problems. But as we cannot predict what will or will not go wrong, it is in the interest of caution and safety that all patients should be admitted to a coronary care unit. It is why I recommended that Bernard should go into hospital *immediately* I diagnosed that he had suffered a heart attack.

Inside the unit

When Bernard arrived inside the unit he was put into bed and then monitored closely. He received an ECG and the nurses observed him closely. The ECG was then monitored by placing three sticky pads to the chest. Unfortunately Bernard is a hairy object so we had to shave part of his chest leaving three bare patches. After this the wires are attached to a monitor. This is a small television-like screen displaying the electrical activity of the heart. There is often an automatic device attached to these machines which will recall any curious electrical activity. Next, a small plastic needle is put into a vein of your arm. We have described that this allows any drugs to be put straight into the veins without an injection. I know that our heroic patient will confirm that it is relatively painless.

Bernard could have been given a mild tranquilliser to relax him; in fact he received some morphine to relieve the severe pain. After that we left him in relative peace for about forty-eight hours apart from regular checks on his blood pressure, temperature and pulse rate. Each day we do a further ECG. This demonstrates exactly what sort of a heart attack the patient has suffered and also where it is located in the heart. Inevitably a number of people will be admitted to a CCU who have not had a heart attack and we cannot be completely certain for up to three days whether the chest pain was a heart attack or a bit of indigestion.

Blood tests

In Bernard's case we also took blood to confirm my initial diagnosis and this is common for all patients in the unit. This is because when the muscle in your heart is deprived of its blood supply the heart muscle cells gradually break up and release a variety of chemicals into the bloodstream. Some of these are enzymes. It is quite easy to measure the quantity of particular enzymes in the blood and if they show a marked rise for a day or two after severe chest pain it will confirm that you have had a heart attack.

Other blood tests may be taken to check your body generally, for example to make sure your kidneys and liver are working properly. Your temperature will be taken and may rise for a few days after your heart attack. No one quite knows why but it is probably related to your body's stress response. In fact once I had received the results of the enzyme test on Bernard's blood it confirmed my earlier diagnosis. There was no doubt he had suffered a heart attack.

Relieving anxiety

I am pleased he pointed out the therapeutic value of the nurses responsible for his care. Most people remember the nurses they meet on the first night because it is a particularly stressful time. The comfort all nursing staff offer a patient is great value. Initially a patient like Bernard will have his anxiety moderated because of the morphine. It not only relieves pain but can make you feel very cheerful. With nurses around you all the time you will feel safe and many people will try and ignore the fact they have been told they have had a heart attack. Notice how Bernard kept wanting to hide the reality of his situation by trying to prove how normal he was. It's only a defence mechanism which some people adopt to stop themselves worrying. Others may do the opposite and ask lots of questions. Everybody is different and believe me Bernard asks question after question. He wants to know every aspect of his case and of course I answer him, and all my patients, as honestly as I can.

Into the ward

You would normally stay in the coronary care unit for about two to three days. That's because complications of a heart attack usually occur in the first forty-eight hours or so. After that any immediate danger rapidly disappears.

Bernard remained in the CCU for two days and then in common with most patients he was transferred to a ward or private room away from special care. The monitor, which shows the action of the heart, is unplugged and although there are plenty of nurses around patients are left to their own devices. This is a positive step, an indication that you are improving and there is no need to be afraid moving out of the relative 'safety' of the CCU.

From now on the improvement is quite rapid. We had very little success keeping Bernard in bed for two days nor could we persuade him to use a bed-pan but normally it is wiser for patients to get up on the third day to use the proper lavatory and to do a little walking. Over the next two or three days patients should be able to walk around quite freely and just before they leave they should try a flight of stairs. Because no two heart attacks are identical this recovery programme may take longer and the length of time of each stage may vary. In addition a lack of staff within the National Health Service is tending to slow things up and a patient might feel he is being discharged too early. I do not believe there is any need to fear this. Remember some people have heart attacks on the bus while on the way to work and don't realise it. Then they rush around as they always have done. The heart is remarkably resilient particularly after the first few days.

Into the future

Future developments of a coronary care unit include the possibility of drugs which may dissolve the clot which is the initial cause of the problem. Anticoagulants, drugs which slow the clotting process, have no effect on clots which have already formed, but two drugs, one called Streptokinase and another called Tissue plasmin activator, actually dissolve the clot. If given quickly enough it seems logical that there might be a proper treatment of a heart attack. Streptokinase is known to clear about one-third of all clots, and tissue plasmin perhaps as much as two-thirds. No one is yet sure of their full potential or whether they will ultimately alter the death rate, but trials are underway and results should become available over the next few years.

And what about our patient? Well you know what he's like when it comes to advice. He tends to ignore it. Bernard left hospital with his booklets explaining what a heart attack was all about, and very strict orders from me. Going home for him was just the beginning of a struggle to make him change his life, with dire warnings of what could happen if he doesn't. We shall see what 'going home' was like (and his wife has my very deepest sympathy).

9. The wounded warrior

BERNARD FALK

Home looked the same. But it felt different. Had I only been away a week? There was the bed where I suffered that terrible pain. That was where my GP and Roger Blackwood had first examined me. It was the first time anyone realised I might be having a heart attack. My clothes were all in place and the family: my wife, baby daughter Rebecca, cats Baggie and Sid, dog Abie, all seemed pleased to see me. I was delighted to surround myself with their comfort and concern and it was high summer. We are lucky enough to have a nice garden with a swimming pool. I live very near a beautiful stretch of the River Thames where I keep a small boat. In all I had to stay at home for six weeks, the longest ever in my life and I looked forward to a happy relaxing time.

There was so much I could do, like all the little jobs around the house which never quite get done because you never have the time. I resolved to occupy my time by cleaning the patio, sorting out my hundreds of books into a sensible library, cataloguing my collection of music tapes and records. I was determined, too, to spend more time with all my children including the three older ones from my former marriage. Remember I felt no pain. I had lost about five pounds in weight during seven days in hospital, so I was in shape to get myself really fit.

But my mind buzzed with questions, largely about my health and the chances of survival. My experience at home turned out to be a mixed bag—part-paradise, part-nightmare, largely a combination of doubt, fear, anxiety, pleasure, and a slow return to both physical and mental normality.

It is not easy. You feel wounded. You know your body is damaged, that you are more vulnerable than before. But mentally you have much more time on your hands to reflect on issues which have always been pushed to the back of your mind in the past. There is the possibility of death. Every last twinge, ache or pain tends to be blown up out of all proportion. Even a sudden stab of pain in the leg is instantly diagnosed by you as a thrombosis leading to another heart attack. The only consolation is to remind yourself that it wasn't fatal the last time and to cling to the reassurances given by the doctors that there is no need to worry.

Almost universally patients like me grab hold of every last bit of information about their condition, and you run through what the doctors have told you over and over again. 'You are going to be all right,' I remembered Roger saying. 'The muscle affected is dead. If you feel another pain it will not be the heart.' After a while it is pointless. You have to learn to live with the problem or else you go round the twist.

In some ways I envy people with religious faith during times of stress and anxiety. I am not afraid of actually dying providing it is relatively quick, and I am fully aware that we must all pop off at some time. But although I was brought up in the Jewish faith I do not believe very much of its spiritual teachings, like the existence of an afterlife, or the concept of heaven and hell. People who do believe must gain great comfort from a faith that teaches that death is not the end. We agnostics or atheists have very little to fall back on except the companionship of people in this life. We are without the guiding hand of a spiritual father, and sometimes we feel lonely.

However for me the first few weeks at home provided a relief from the slogging routine of work. I pushed business or professional worries into the back of my mind. There were more important things to consider—like what to cook for lunch, when I dare drive the car, the distance I could walk without feeling tired—humdrum activities which I had never bothered about before. And being at home is certainly an eye-opener, particularly for a husband used to spending so little time in it during daylight hours.

In business or during your life at work you usually come across a breed of people who in recent years have become universally known as Wallies. They are the clots who infest your life by regularly committing acts of crass stupidity. A Wally is the bus driver who puts his foot down as the old lady struggles towards the stop. A Wally is the secretary who spills nail-varnish all over the only copy of the Chairman's report the morning of the Annual General Meeting. A Wally is the office boy who trips over the computer cable and puts the entire system out of action. These people are all standard business-type Wallies. But at home the Wally takes on a quite astonishing professional status.

I quickly discovered that you meet more Wallies per minute at home than you can meet in a lifetime at work. Furthermore because they prey on housewives their Walliness reaches appalling levels of arrogance. They know they are Wallies and they are proud of it. In the few weeks I spent at home they arrived at the house at regular intervals determined to drive me totally round the bend.

There was a man who arrived to fix the roof. He put his foot through three good tiles leaving a gaping hole. Another clown came to fix the pump for the swimming-pool. He took the pump off to clean it and couldn't put it back together again.

Then a central heating engineer came to fix the pipes. The water from one cascaded all over a new carpet leaving a soggy patch. When I complained by banging my head against the wall he said, 'Them carpets are very bad quality, Guv. If you want a new one my brother's in the trade.'

The classic Wally was the man I hired to drive me around the neighbourhood when after a couple of weeks I was allowed away from the domestic nest. He crashed my car into another car causing £2,000 worth of damage. A day later he resigned because he said his nerves couldn't stand the strain of crashing cars any longer.

Finally I myself had the privilege of joining all these highly proficient Wallies by committing an act of such Walliness that it should have earned me a place as President of the World International Wally Congress. I drilled a hole through the main water pipe while fitting a plastic cup holder to a tile in the main bathroom.

Yes I confess. I did it. The water came out of the wall like a rocket-propelled jet. An emergency plumber was summoned by my wife, while I was forced to stand like the little boy at the Dutch dyke with my finger on the hole in the pipe.

When he arrived I said, 'We were lucky getting a plumber like you at such short notice on a Saturday.'

He said, 'It's our busiest time, Sir, due to all the Wallies drilling holes in the wall.'

Then things really hotted up. He knocked out three tiles to repair the pipe, and left, leaving three gaps where the tiles used to be. I knocked out two other tiles trying to get three replacement tiles on to the empty spaces on the wall. In doing that I managed to bang my thumb with a hammer. It is an interesting economic statistic to reveal that the plastic cup holder cost £2.50. It cost £265 and a damaged thumb to try and put it up. In fact it is still not up. I have five gaps in the wall waiting for tiles that have to be specially made, shipped, imported and paid for in Italy.

So if you believe that being at home is likely to alleviate stress, then forget it. There is more stress in the domestic environment than you ever face at work. During my five weeks at home I nearly burst a blood vessel with the constant aggravation and God knows what it did to the relationship with my wife. [See Mrs Falk's exposé on p. 133.]

On a more serious note, apart from the physical damage to your heart, there are major psychological problems to be overcome during this rehabilitation period. For the first few weeks you are meant to rest and take things easy. But because you don't feel ill you have to restrain yourself from overdoing things. For two weeks you are meant to confine yourself to the home and garden and to spend a few hours every afternoon in bed. I found myself getting up at six or seven in the morning as usual, pottering around the house and then I was like a caged lion wondering what to do.

In other words you have the problem of learning to relax, of forgetting the outside world and sinking yourself into the cocoon of a life without stress. That's what I discovered but then I have an 'A' personality which probably led me into a heart attack in the first place.

Hobbies helped. I built some model aircraft but abandoned that after spilling plastic cement all over the carpet in the study. Cleaning out a spare room occupied some time, until I scraped a hole in the wallpaper with a ladder. I tried cleaning the boat but when I put my foot through a plastic container and acid burned a hole in the bottom I began to feel that it was remotely possible I was a downright liability at home. [I refer you to Mrs Falk, Mrs Falk's mother, Thameside Police, Maidenhead Fire Brigade, Thames Water Conservancy, if you want more details.]

Physically I was delighted that one of Roger's recommendations during a rehabilitation period is to start walking for short distances after only two weeks at home, building up to about two miles over the entire programme. I have always felt comfortable with walking. You simply put one foot in front of the other and repeat the process until you stop, sit down and resolve never to bother walking again. But this was the first time I have had the luxury of being able to spend long periods walking. Where I live provides some of the loveliest walks you could imagine. And believe me once you start walking you can go really mad and break into a trot. Soon you would find yourself jogging, having another heart attack, and starting the thing all over again.

Enter Abie. Abie is a Jewish dog. He doesn't realise he's Jewish. In reality he's a German Munsterlander, which is a kind of mix between an Irish Retriever, a Bulgarian Pointer and a Right Mess. But as his ancient forebears were German I thought it only appropriate that he should be given a Jewish name in honour of my ancient forebears. It also enables me to yell, 'Abie, Valkies', when I take him for a romp along the towpath. I mention Abie because I believe a dog is a great incentive for a clapped-out cardiac patient to get some exercise.

During my period at home Abie couldn't believe his luck. During the third week, when I was allowed out of the house and garden, I got up at seven in the morning to walk Abie along the footpath which runs beside the Cliveden Reach on the River Thames. ['This is a rotten fib,' writes Mrs Falk. 'I had to force them both out by threatening to hide his whisky.'] Forget that intrusion. Once out breathing in the magnificent fresh air and mosquitoes we took a brisk 200-yard stroll to the boat house where Abie would piddle all over the freshly painted verandah, then up a quiet country lane where Abie would attempt to eat a hedgehog, and on to a side road where Abie would attempt to eat a neighbour's Corgi, and home—

So if you believe that being at home is
likely to alleviate stress, then forget it . . .

knackered and bunged up with stress. The distance is about half a mile.

I repeated the same in the afternoon ['This is another fib,' writes Mrs Falk. 'He used to try and slope off to the pub.'] Ignore her, she gets her own bit in a minute. But soon I found myself getting stronger and more confident about taking exercise. This is important. At first you feel a little frightened to exert your body at all in case you drop down dead with another heart attack. But with every step of a brisk walk you feel psychologically stronger, particularly as in my case exercise did not induce any pain. For this reason I am very grateful to Abie, who did wonders for my stress by chasing other dogs, crapping on my neighbours' immaculate lawns and playing Bullies and Cowards with the postman. Of course I am not suggesting every cardiac patient should get a dog but for some people it can help. If you want to live to be a ripe old age, however, I recommend that you should stay away from German Jewish Munsterlanders who answer to the call, 'Valkies' . . . on my life.

Finally, in between dealing with Wallies, irate neighbours, crashed cars, and a rapidly deteriorating marital relationship, I began to realise that each day had to be taken as it came. In misery. I'm only joking. For someone like me it is a severe shock to the system to discover that each day demands the sort of intelligence and concentration that you find at a meeting of the Arthur Scargill Fan Club. Nowt. And a bored patient is an irritating object to be near. [See Mrs Falk's exposé.]

In fact the weeks passed quickly, like The Hundred Years War, until it became time to consider a return to work. The initial convalescence was over, or at least the first stage. Ahead lay a series of medical tests which would establish what was wrong with my heart, the level of damage caused and what action had to be taken to safeguard my health in the future. Also ahead lay the challenge of resuming work and the problems I would face in not returning to my old lifestyle. Physically I was pretty fit, nearly a stone lighter and I had stopped smoking. Mentally, well that's another matter. It takes time for the psychological scars of a heart attack to heal and in my case they are still mending.

In spite of all the rude things she is about to say about me

I remain grateful to my wife for all she did to make those weeks of rehabilitation a little easier. The crowning moment came when I heard a whispered conversation going on down the telephone in the living-room.

Respecting other people's privacy is not my strong point so I placed a big ear next to the keyhole and heard my beloved wife talking to . . . not her lover. Worse: my ex-wife. Guess who was the subject of the conversation? Later in some indignation I asked what all that had been about. Normally they have as much in common with one another as Little Noddy and Attila the Hun. 'I think your first wife has got it made,' she said. 'You keep her but she doesn't have to live with you.' Clearly there was something wrong. Could it be she actually wanted me to go to work?

LINDA FALK

(dictated under duress)

The wounded warrior is a pain in the neck

I have been waiting a long time for this. A whole section to get my own back and state exactly what I think without HIM breathing down my neck. I had to put up with him at home for five weeks and it should have been a wonderful chance for him to relax with his family. But immediately he got home Bernard insisted on doing things, none of them productive or even useful. But he cannot keep still. He gets bored so quickly. He cannot relax and that puts pressure on everyone else. In fact I know how Bernard gets rid of his stress. He's such a pain in the neck that he passes it on to everyone else.

I don't know how many women married to men who suffered heart attacks would agree with this but for much of the time when Bernard was at home he was pure hell, hell on earth. He's pretty awful under normal circumstances but when he suffered his heart attack it was as if all his normal characteristics, like wanting his way all the time, became even more accentuated.

He just doesn't understand what it's like being married to someone like him. For a start you hardly ever see him. He only needs about five hours' sleep and for six days a week we never see each other before he goes to work.

Believe it or not he usually leaves the house about 6.30 a.m. and then that's it for the day. Now most husbands starting work that early would come home in time to spend a little time with their family. Not Bernard. He sits around in his office talking and drinking with his cronies and then rolls in at round about 8 o'clock at night. Then he wants a big meal, which is bad for him at that time of night, and just as I am about to tell him about *my* day there's a nasty snoring noise coming from the couch and the blighter has dropped off.

He also works on a Saturday morning doing his radio show and he's no sooner back in the house when he disappears off to the pub. In the afternoon he sleeps it off while I take the children and the dog for a walk. Don't believe all that rubbish he wrote about walking with Abie along the river. I do that. He hates walking and he's always beastly to Abie anyway. And you really ought to know that this was our life *before* he had his heart attack. It was even worse when he came home from hospital.

My husband is no little soldier. Wounded warrior! If he gets a cold he thinks he's dying and makes everyone else know it. If ever Roger Blackwood wants to start a rehabilitation clinic for wives, then I'll be the first customer. For a start Bernard will never listen to any advice. If you give him any advice he ignores it and does exactly what he wants anyway. It's like talking to a deaf door-post. To my intense irritation he has mastered the art of appearing to listen to what I'm saying to him when his mind is miles away.

He even nods from time to time as if he's giving me his full attention but I know it's really gone in one ear and out of the other. What's even more maddening is that most of the time I am only trying to protect him from himself. For years now I have been telling him to lose weight and eat properly. I've tried to set a good example. At home we have low-fat spread instead of butter. He goes out to the supermarket and buys butter. I tell him to eat sensibly, a small amount for breakfast, a little more for lunch and something light for dinner. No! He knows better. He starves himself all day and then staggers home half-drunk or completely drunk and gobbles down a gigantic meal just before he goes to bed or drops off on the couch. I beg him to eat more fish, vegetables and chicken. He loves big steaks, spicy curries, Chinese feasts, in fact just about everything that's bad for him. His favourite meal is a huge fry-up: eggs, bacon, chops, sausage, chips etc. Tell him that all the grease is bad for him and I get accused of nagging.

Then there's his pathological obsession with avoiding any form of exericise. He should go for lots of walks or do some cycling. Instead he goes down to the towpath and teaches Abie to chase joggers. I have joined no less than two excellent health clubs ['EXPENSIVE health clubs which cost me a packet,' writes Bernard, unable to restrain himself any more.] But ask him to come swimming, go for a brisk walk with the dog, do some exercises at home, and a blank look comes over his face and, before you know where you are, he's disappeared off to the pub again.

On a more serious note, when he was at home during the five weeks' rehabilitation period, he became a very different character. In spite of all I've said about him Bernard is a good-natured man, very warm and human and with a great sense of humour. But after his heart attack the slightest thing made him irritable. He snapped and shouted over the most trivial matters. I suspect it was because he felt pretty hurt inside anyway, not so much damaged physically, but as though he had been struck down right in the prime of his life. I kept wondering if he was really scared of dying young like his father. But you can never tell with Bernard.

On the surface he always seems cheerful and maybe he hides the real fear which lies inside? Also I think he suddenly felt a bit inadequate, which is ridiculous really, and I firmly believe there is a terrible onus upon wives to keep reassuring their husbands that they love them and everything is going to be all right. The reality of course is that we all know he works hard to keep all of us including his ex-wife (lucky girl) and a total of five children. He loves his work and spends far too much time at it. But take that away from Bernard and you would destroy the thing that makes him tick.

In spite of that when he was at home for five weeks we nearly left it for good. He cooks. In fact he's a very good cook. But Bernard cooks as though he had three hundred servants. It takes hours to scrape off all the grease on the cooker, get the floor cleaned and sort out the general mess he leaves, and when he was at home he cooked *three times a day*.

Looking after him and cleaning up his mess was a full-time job. On top of that he's one of those blokes who cannot even knock a nail in properly. He rushes everything. He's not methodical (what man is?) and to my horror he decided to do lots of little jobs around the house. When he gets out his electric drill my heart sinks. If pre-warned I can get the plumbers and electricians standing by and always we have to call a man in to repair Bernard's efforts at do-it-yourself. You can imagine the cost when he was around and about with his blinking nails, hammer and drill every day for five weeks.

It sounds of course as though I am heading straight for a divorce. He always says there's no point in that because he hasn't got any money left after his first divorce and if I sound just a bit complaining let me put the record straight. Men have to realise what it is like to be married to someone really selfish. People like Bernard believe the entire world revolves around them. Remember when he had his heart attack I was six-and-a-half months pregnant with a very demanding two-year-old toddler to cope with. When Bernard had his heart attack my baby stopped growing for a couple of weeks because of all the worry and stress. Thankfully Hannah is now a beautiful, healthy girl. But when he got home Bernard wanted all my attention. He needed pampering and forgot that a wife simply cannot abandon her children no matter how sick her husband is.

Oh! I ought to mention one thing. Bernard is a superlative breadwinner. All his dependants, and there are more of them every year, do extremely well, which is why he works so hard to keep us. And there's just another little thing I ought to mention which might seem a bit odd after writing the way I have.

We all love him very much indeed and want to keep him. The prospect of losing him is the most awful thought in the world. Selfish sod.

BERNARD FALK

Note That entire section was a load of old codswallop and the reader can be forgiven for ignoring it and racing on to the good bits which follow.

DR ROGER BLACKWOOD

There is no doubt that after a heart attack the heart heals faster than the brain. But in this section I want to deal with general guidance for those who have experienced a heart attack and their families. This rehabilitation period of recovery is crucial.

The psychological blow experienced by a patient can vary considerably. Unlike Bernard who is a resilient character, some people never return to work, more because of fear than because of medical problems with their heart. This is sad because this fear is often not necessary. As I have already explained, a heart attack is like a broken leg and takes about six weeks to heal. At that stage everyone should be well on the way to living a normal life again.

There is a tendency to assume that a heart attack is the result of an improper diet, smoking, alcohol, obesity, a lack of medical care, particularly if the patient was completely fit before it happened. So the only way to help a patient at this stage is to explain everything about a heart attack simply and repeatedly. This happened with Bernard although he neglects to mention it. On the surface he always seemed cheerful and optimistic but I suspected that he was suffering from quite considerable anxiety and fear, and we spent some time discussing why most of his worries were unnecessary. In fact when they are in hospital many patients try to convince themselves they have not had a heart attack at all, and they ignore all the advice.

Going home can be frightening because quite suddenly the 'experts' are not on hand and one can feel very lonely indeed. In addition, the full impact of what has happened does not dawn on some patients until they have got home, and this makes them even more frightened. It is curious that witnessing another patient having a cardiac arrest in hospital may be less frightening than suddenly realising that you have had a heart attack once you are back at home. It is quite normal for a patient to feel anxiety and depression for a few weeks. But this soon passes and is seldom severe. What the patient needs at this stage is reassurance from a doctor, and a GP, who will have received your case history from the hospital or specialist, is in a good position to provide this help.

Physical symptoms

There are physical symptoms which can occur after a heart attack, but there is no need for anyone to become anxious. A heart attack patient needs rest and that applies to their mental attitude as well as the physical side. When the patient goes home, he may get depressed and anxious, and these feelings are often accentuated by curious flitting pains. These only last for a short while; they are quite common and occur in a variety of places in the chest. They are caused by a spasm of the breathing muscles between the ribs and come most frequently when a patient is resting.

Tiredness is another common symptom. This is caused by the heart attack itself, the psychological stress such an experience creates and because in hospital there is so little physical activity.

In addition you may be feeling breathless and aware of your heart beating. This is caused almost entirely by high levels of adrenalin in your body. When there is underlying anxiety the body produces large quantities of adrenalin, which puts muscle on edge. If your breathing muscles are on edge your chest will feel tight and you will have a sensation of breathlessness. If your heart muscle is on edge it will beat more strongly and you will feel an uncomfortable thumping. Indeed, some of the chest pains will be produced by the same method, a spasm of the chest muscles. It is easy to see how an underlying, somewhat unexpected anxiety can lead to symptoms which in turn lead to further worry and anxiety. I hope post-cardiac patients like Bernard realise that all these symptoms are completely normal and easily explained.

Rehabilitation

It is at this stage that people like Bernard think of a rehabilitation programme. There is no better opportunity to change someone's lifestyle. Future illness may be avoided by the correct approach at this stage. Remember the words of Dr Lawrence Wood: 'The most powerful of all medical and paramedic personnel is the patient, highly motivated, not costing anything, even willing to pay.' Of course much of this will also apply to the patient's spouse.

The essence of a rehabilitation programme is physical activity and psychological counselling. The latter is obvious in its need and involves basically reassurance and education. But why bother with the physical side? Surely the patient will recover anyway? In hospital when a patient spends a lot of time in bed there is a 20 to 30 per cent decrease in physical work capacity after a short period of immobility. The volume of blood reduces by about a pint after ten days' rest and this will only be restored by returning to exercise.

The less mobile you are the more prone you are to clots in the bloodstream. There is also a modest decrease in lung capacity as well as some breakdown of muscle, reducing its strength. Physical exercise is therefore important and can return you to normal quite quickly.

There is no evidence that rehabilitation programmes prolong life but there is little doubt that those who receive both physical training and psychological advice are much better adapted to a decent quality of life in the long run.

Two particular factors of psychological counselling were emphasised in an important study from Oxford:

The patients who did best were those who had resumed sexual relations with their regular partner soon after their heart attack. This should be within three to four weeks and has very important psychological benefits particularly in men.

The other particular benefit to emerge was advice to the husband or wife not to mollycoddle the patient. There is a tendency for a wife to over-protect the patient and prevent him from doing even the smallest tasks, like washing-up. This undermines his self-confidence by constantly reminding him of what has happened.

Rehabilitation is very important but surprisingly few hospitals offer the service to patients. That's first because no one is quite sure who should run it—the doctor, the physiotherapy department or the psychologist. Secondly, there is no financial provision for it. The few programmes that do exist have to run on charity. Thirdly, it is not thought to be really medical, more like social work. Whatever the merits or demerits of this, the fact is that few people will be offered the privilege of a course.

There are also huge demands on the time of a consultant cardiologist who would normally initiate such a course. Each district general hospital has up to 500,000 residents. They can produce between 1,000 and 2,000 attacks a year. Each district has *only one* consultant.

He or she would have to set up a rehabilitation programme in addition to looking after all the inpatients and outpatients. Suppose the cardiologist gave 30 minutes a week to each patient for the first six weeks after their heart attack? This would be 3,000 hours of work a year. A consultant working 'normal' hours per week has only got about 2,000 a year. So to create an ideal environment for a large national rehabilitation programme we would need many more cardiologists. Instead many hospital patients have to make do with a booklet explaining what a heart attack is and an exercise programme written on a piece of paper. It is clearly unsatisfactory and one of the major reasons why I decided to co-operate in writing this book.

What happens at home?

Every consultant has a slightly different rehabilitation programme but this is what I recommend. First I give each patient a booklet which explains what a heart attack is. It is called *You and Your Heart Attack*, and answers most of the important questions.

Next I give the patient a programme for the five weeks they *must* spend at home after leaving hospital. Bernard is clearly a law unto himself. He was engaged in a lot of activities almost immediately he got home. I know he drove his car before he should have done and my spies in his house also report that he disappeared off to the pub far too soon for the good of his health. So let us ignore his example and examine what I recommend for a rehabilitation programme.

THE REHABILITATION PROGRAMME

WEEK 1. At home in the house only. The patient can climb the stairs to bed and come down in the morning. He (She) should sit around most of the time and have a rest after lunch.

WEEK 2. House and garden. Assuming the garden is not fifty acres, the patient can walk in his house and garden fairly freely. This is limited in cold weather which can put a significant strain on the heart. In the winter a more active day in the house is all that can be achieved. Visitors may call as long as the patient wishes them to. A good excuse to keep out unwanted guests at this stage is the usual white lie—'The doctor says he's not to have visitors yet.'

WEEK 3. House, garden and half a mile to a mile's walk each day. It is surprising how few people take even a half-mile walk a day as exercise, and at first it can be quite tiring. *It is important that your wife/husband or friend accompany you in case you feel unwell.* In the house odd jobs of a light nature can be done, like wiring a plug, typing, playing cards. If you are organised you can avoid washing-up, but you must not feel too fragile or be scared of these jobs. Wives who have had heart attacks can now do such jobs as vacuum-cleaning and gentle hand-washing.

WEEK 4. House, garden and a mile to a mile and a half walk a day. You should now be rehabilitating fast. In particular you can resume sexual relations. This is tactfully said to be 'with a regular partner'. Careful studies have been made of sexual intercourse. With a regular partner we are told that the sexual act takes sixteen minutes twice a week with an orgasm lasting fifteen seconds. This is the physical equivalent of walking about half a mile followed by climbing two flights of stairs. If you can manage this then you can 'make love'. What happens with your occasional partner (mistress, lover, prostitute) is anybody's guess but you may well end up with five or six flights of stairs. Such a situation would be inappropriate at this stage.

Driving—At this stage it is probably permissible to drive but only after consultation with your own doctor. The DVLC suggest waiting eight weeks and this would certainly be safer.

But if your heart attack is uncomplicated an earlier start with short distances may be permissible.

WEEK 5. House, garden and a two-mile walk every day. You should be returning pretty well to normal at this stage except for not working. Perhaps a four-hour visit to the office, factory or workplace just to reassure everyone, yourself included, that you have made a good recovery.

WEEK 6. Return to work.

Pills and medicine

There is a natural curiosity to know what tablets you are taking and what they are for. In Bernard's case I prescribed Beta-Blockers and a diuretic and it is worthwhile examining the pills and medicines in case some patients are confused about their purpose.

Beta-Blockers
These are the most widely used of all tablets after a heart attack. They literally block the effect of adrenalin on the heart and in doing so act as a 'brake' on its actions. They reduce the force of contraction of the heart and so lower the blood pressure. Also they reduce the heart rate so that when sitting the pulse is around 50/55 beats per minute and not the normal 70/75 beats per minute. These two actions allow the heart to work at a slow pace and use up less energy. They are useful after a heart attack for high blood pressure, angina or palpitations. In addition they have been shown to cut down the death rate after a heart attack at least in certain circumstances.

Like all medicine the prescribing of drugs for each particular patient is an individual decision on the doctor's part, so one cannot generalise about who should have what tablet and for how long. Tablets are never handed out like Smarties because they all have side-effects. Beta-Blockers can exacerbate asthma and make your hands and feet very cold. In addition many patients say that they feel 'weary and dreary' whilst on these tablets. Nevertheless they are of immense value and one of the greatest advances in medicine in the last forty years. A good example of their effectiveness is that Bernard has not reported any side-effects whatsoever since he has been taking Beta-Blockers.

Diuretic or water pill
This is another commonly used pill after a heart attack. These tablets make you pass much more urine than you normally would, draining the body of excess fluid. If the heart does not pump as strongly as it should after an attack extra fluid accumulates in all parts of the body. When there is too much water on the lungs breathlessness develops when you exert yourself. Much of the water gradually passes down the body producing swollen ankles. The water pill removes the excess water and makes you feel much better.

There are many types of these tablets, Lasix (last six hours) and Burinex (better urine excretion) being the most common. These tablets have the side-effect of lowering the body's potassium levels. This is a salt which will make you feel very weak and lethargic if not maintained at proper levels, therefore you will also be given potassium pills to take.

Other drugs
Digoxin may also be prescribed. It is interesting because its main component, digitalis, has been used for over 200 years. It is derived from the foxglove and is a heart tonic, although its action is relatively weak except in controlling the heart rate and preventing it from going too fast.

Some patients will be given other tablets to control their heart rate. When the heart is irregular or fast the patient will feel fluttering or thumping in the chest which is most uncomfortable. Such drugs as Disopyramide, Veramil, Flecainide, Amiodarone and Beta-Blockers can be given for this.

Drugs to prevent blood clots
Occasionally a clot can form in your leg veins after a heart attack. This is usually caused by inactivity and lying in bed and is treated by *anticoagulants*. These are tablets which slow down the rate at which blood clots. They do not 'thin' blood as many people think nor do they prevent the blood from ever clotting. They slow the rate of clotting by about two or three times. Blood normally clots in about 13 seconds. On anticoagu-

lants your dosage is adjusted so that your blood clots in 30–40 seconds.

The usual tablet used is Warfarin (also rat poison) which has no real side-effects at all but does interact with certain drugs such as aspirin and alcohol and this means that you have to be rather careful while taking them. A blood test is needed from time to time to check the rate of blood clotting so as to get the correct dose of Warfarin.

Women

Heart attacks tend to be male-orientated because in middle age heart attacks in men outnumber the women by 2 to 1. It is very difficult for many women when they return home because very often their husbands expect them to start running the household fairly quickly, particularly if there are young children around. Fortunately this is uncommon because wives tend to be older (55 years plus) when they have a heart attack. If your husband is the sort who expects to be waited on hand and foot, it may be sensible to go and stay with your grown-up daughter or daughter-in-law for a couple of weeks after leaving hospital.

Travel

Driving a car is permissible after three or four weeks and travel by air after about six weeks. The cabin pressure of most aeroplanes is the equivalent of about 5,000 feet and at this level the oxygen is at a normal level.

Jobs

Jobs range from sedentary to heavy manual. A man at a desk job would clearly return to work much more quickly than a coal-face worker. Returning to work should start after around six weeks but it is essential to take your doctor's advice.

Some patients will have their own business which they think will collapse if they are not there. This is rarely the case but it is true that these patients may worry much more if they don't stay in contact with their jobs. It is sensible to use the phone to keep things 'ticking over' during the weeks at home so that their anxiety is reduced.

In Bernard's case he spent a week in hospital and five weeks at home before returning to work. Ahead of him lay several extremely important visits to the outpatients department of the hospital and after that we decided to examine the inside of his heart to discover his true condition. I shall deal with this in more detail in the next chapter.

Family support

Linda Falk describes quite graphically the early days after Bernard's heart attack and while I am sure they are both very deeply attached to one another, clearly her outburst shows the strain they both suffered. This 'life crisis' is a mixture of uncertainty and fear coupled with a frustration at not being able to deal with a medical problem directly or to 'get it over with'. Anyone who has met Bernard will know of the enormous energy he exudes so he must be difficult to live with at the best of times.

After a heart attack all normal problems are compounded by fear and depression, perhaps worse than doctors generally believe. Fear and depression create insecurity, hence Bernard's selfish desire to know that he was still loved and a 'very important person'. Jealousy begins to creep into a relationship if a husband feels inadequate and even children can become rivals in a wounded husband's desire for attention and affection.

Bernard wanted to know he was still needed. Sitting at home doing odd jobs very badly hardly helps the ego and can keep up the fear. It is good if these household functions help to change your lifestyle but ultimately people can die of fear if it gets too excessive. Reassurance and a constant reminder of what the doctor has said about your condition is very important and if the news is good, as in Bernard's case, it should be repeated time and time again.

Linda complains that Bernard ignored all her advice and she knew that a heart attack was inevitable. How many times have I heard that before from a spouse? It is a simple fact that your wife or your husband often knows you better than you know yourself. They are the best possible people to give sound advice provided, unlike Bernard, you are prepared to listen. Bernard will have told himself to stop smoking on many occasions but he should have listened to Linda about that and about his diet and his workload and, if he had, he might have avoided his heart attack.

Amongst the many emotions one feels after a heart attack is anger followed by remorse so partners should try to avoid the 'I-told-you-so' attitude. All that does is to make you very lonely indeed.

What couples must try to do is talk at great length. They must sort out any problems together and it will surprise a heart attack victim how understanding a partner can be. Sharing problems eases the burden enormously and I know Linda was immensely supportive to Bernard. She is quite a character and I suspect this 'life crisis' has had at least one benefit—it has brought them closer together.

One of the arguments a man and wife are most likely to have after a heart attack is about exactly what the doctor did say. Even when you see a couple together there will be differences of interpretation. So try to make sure when you see your doctor that everything is quite clear. Filling in time during the few weeks of recovery is quite an arduous task and many people who have had a coronary will rush ahead of the rehabilitation programme I have described. Within reason this is not too bad. The quicker you get back to a normal routine the better you will feel.

So there is no easy way out of a heart attack for the family as a whole. Support from everyone—friends, relatives, neighbours, doctors—is crucial, along with a rehabilitation programme wherever possible.

Religious comfort

I occasionally hear patients say that a heart attack has been brought upon them because they have 'sinned against God'. However people can turn to God during a time of crisis. In counselling patients on this subject I suggest that religious faith is not such a bad thing. If you can come to terms with death—and that is the only certain event of life—then life itself becomes much easier to cope with.

This is not to say that you rely on religion to provide a cure rather than doing something positive about changing your lifestyle. No one wants to die and leave loved ones behind, but religious faith can help to soften fear and relieve stress. Few doctors ever mention the religious side of a patient's life. If we are to deal with the whole person religion should not be ignored. It can bring people immense comfort.

10. The outpatient and back to work

BERNARD FALK

The National Heart Hospital is a gaunt Victorian pile near Harley Street, in the West End of London. On the day I first went there as an outpatient it looked like Clapham Junction railway station during the rush hour. You simply couldn't move for people. Scheduled to be replaced by a modern building within the next few years, it is having to cope with the worst epidemic of heart disease in British medical history. Today the major problem is overcrowding. There are too many heart patients fitting into too little space. Working in these conditions are the staff, who in my view should go to the top of every honours list for their skilled devotion to the poor wretches who walk or are carried through their doors. That's the commercial over. It's no worse off than any other NHS hospital in an era when Britain has more millionaire business-men than ever before and pays its doctors and nurses among the lowest wages in Europe. Interesting isn't it that a twenty-five-year-old financial whizz-kid in the City can earn up to £250,000 a year serving the well-heeled investment community. If he had a heart attack through overwork, his life might be saved by young medical staff earning wages only a fraction above the official poverty line.

Whatever the rights and wrongs, if you are treated at the National Heart Hospital, you will receive some of the best specialist expertise in the world, while searching for a place to sit down. When I arrived as an outpatient some cardiac patients were actually sitting on the waiting-room floor because all the seats were taken. I was sent there by Roger Blackwood who wanted to take advantage of its excellent medical facilities and to seek a second opinion on my condition from a fellow soulmate, consultant cardiologist, Dr Kim Fox.

Following the five-week rest and rehabilitation period at

home the time had come for a more thorough examination of my heart. The doctors wanted to know the extent of the damage, the exact location of the blood clot which caused the original attack, the level of cholesterol in my blood and how I would face up to some pretty stringent exercise tests to establish what my heart was like under physical pressure. In that way they would know if I had angina, the narrowing of arteries usually caused by fatty deposits. Following this assessment I would enter the hospital for a few days for an angiogram, an internal examination of the heart. Only then could Blackwood and Fox decide how to treat me with the variety of options at their disposal, ranging from drugs, bypass surgery and, in the rarest of cases, even transplants. Therefore you can imagine that I arrived as an outpatient with a considerable amount of trepidation.

Before you enjoy the thought of me pounding up and down a treadmill it is worth pausing a moment to analyse how a heart patient feels in the period when he is returning to a more normal life. The problem I faced for six to seven weeks after my heart attack was the casual attitude of my doctors towards any form of treatment. I was not being neglected. They knew that there was a blood clot which closed or partially closed an artery. This in turn killed off a portion of my heart muscle. But apart from taking Beta-Blockers and a diuretic pill each day, I had really been left to my own devices. That's because in the majority of cases you cannot actually offer any treatment except for complete rest, and cutting the patient off from any severe stress or strain. So until I went to the hospital as an outpatient I felt as though I was living in a vacuum. What had gone wrong? How badly damaged was my heart? Would I have to undergo an operation? How long did I have to live? Should I make a will? Elementary stuff but I found the rehabilitation period a difficult time.

I was bursting with questions but the doctors were not in a position to answer them until they conducted the tests six weeks after the attack. I found myself wondering about simple, elementary things. Should I wallpaper the living-room? Perhaps not because I might not live long enough to see it. This is an extremely dangerous time. You can suffer from severe depression. In extreme cases patients might lose the will to fight. This leads to an apathy about their condition and health which in turn could lead to a return to smoking, drinking and excessive eating.

I found the only answer was to pour out my anxieties to Roger and to confide in my wife and close friends. The cardiologist must have thought he was fulfilling the role of a psychiatrist rather than a doctor, catering for the terrors of the mind rather than the weaknesses of the body.

So with that background you can imagine my feelings when I arrived at the National Heart Hospital for the tests. I was going to get some answers and kept my fingers crossed that the results would be good. They did all the normal things: take a blood sample, a urine sample, blood pressure, pulse and temperature and an ECG while I was lying down. Then came the exercise test, the first major assessment of my heart's condition. This was determined by putting me through severe physical effort.

For a stress ECG you stand on a treadmill machine which is geared to a wide variety of speeds and movements. A technician and a doctor monitor your progress on ECG equipment which will show any signs of strain or potential danger to the heart. Each stage lasts three minutes and then they take your blood pressure. So off I went on Stage I (there are seven altogether and the machine will go up to an eighth stage for people like Daley Thompson, Frank Bruno and my 83-year-old mum). At first the pace you step along the treadmill is like a slow walk. Then to the next stage and the speed quickens. Halfway through that you begin to puff a little and sweat slightly but there is still very little strain.

But by the time you reach Stage 3 it is like running up a hill backwards carrying a heavy suitcase. My little fat legs were pounding along while my eyes nearly popped out of my head with effort. The sweat streamed off my face. My calf muscles kept screaming, 'Stop you idiot, this is more work than we've done for years.' But still the clock kept ticking, far too slowly. I longed for the machine to stop and suddenly it did. I had reached the end of Stage 3. The medics decided that was enough, but as I stepped off I felt as though the entire world's troubles had been lifted from my shoulders.

THERE WAS NO PAIN IN MY HEART

The ECG was normal, meaning that my heart had not acted abnormally when under physical pressure. Stage 3 (and later I was to reach the end of Stage 4) is not bad. I am hardly going to run a marathon for a bit but it indicated that I could lead a normal life; it was safe to take lots of exercise. Above all it indicated that apart from the original damage the rest of the heart was likely to be fit and healthy. Maybe I'll draw a pension yet.

Dr Kim Fox is an extremely good-natured individual. For a cardiologist he even has a sense of humour. Contemplating the overweight and sweating patient in front of him he took my case history, examined the ECG and pronounced that he was well-satisfied with the results of the exercise test. I left that overcrowded hospital as though I was walking out of Buckingham Palace.

It was the first time since my heart attack that I actually had the confidence to face life squarely in the face. I thought to myself: The odds are good that I will live. I can recover.

Ignoring a passing taxi I briskly walked the one and a half miles back to my office. It was raining and I couldn't have cared less.

I had returned to work a week earlier and immediately become a source of irritation to everyone. I was back and acted as though I wanted to prove I was still in charge even if my heart was a little wonky. For a brief period I stomped around my office waving my stubby arms about and stamping up and down like Napoleon. In fact a model of the diminutive Corsican was left on my desk by an angry workmate and if that hurt a bit then it's no more than I deserved. I suppose I was trying to prove something, that the business couldn't run without me, that things had got slack during my six weeks away. In reality I was trying to bolster my own badly deflated ego and if this means that heart patients are difficult to live with at times then I can only apologise to my loyal hard-working colleagues and hope they understand that sometimes the emotions of a recovering cardiac patient are very difficult to control.

Gradually I began to behave with more patience and toler-ance. Today I hope I am easier to live and work with. As time went by so my confidence began to return and as the tests progressed I began to receive more factual evidence which set my mind at rest.

This followed a further stay at the National Heart Hospital, this time to receive an angiogram. Under a local anaesthetic the doctors enter a probe into the arteries of the heart which shows up its condition. A dye illustrates the flow of blood and the entire progress is shown live on a television screen and is recorded for closer scrutiny later.

Prior to my angiogram I had to spend a day as a patient in one of the wards and for the first time I had a chance to meet other cardiac patients like myself. For me it was a considerable shock and it made me feel far less sorry for myself. Unless you come into contact with the living evidence of the Twentieth-Century Disease, as it's been called, you cannot begin to understand the scale of the problem, and the human misery it can cause. In a heart hospital everyone is there for the same reason. They have something wrong with their heart, but the degrees to which people's lives are affected, or ruined, vary enormously.

I hope my fellow patients will forgive this peep into their lives but I do it to demonstrate the sheer scale of this escalating human tragedy, the disease which afflicts 400,000 people a year in Britain and kills nearly 200,000. I have changed some of their names.

Tony was in the next bed to mine: a warm, kind man born in Goa, the Portuguese-speaking part of India. He was 39, married with a little girl, and was a fitter by trade.

He couldn't move more than a few yards without pain or gasping for breath. His heart was barely functioning at all, thereby affecting other vital organs. He had been waiting for over six months for a heart transplant and as one of the very few people in the country to receive this last-ditch, radical form of treatment he was a bit of a celebrity in the ward, particularly as the famous surgeon Mr Yacoub was going to perform the operation.

Can you imagine what it must feel like to lie in a hospital for months, never knowing whether each day would bring you an operation which reaches into the very frontiers of surgical practice? What it must be like to know that your chances of survival must depend on someone else dying, probably a young person too, in a car crash? Tony is one of the most courageous men I have ever met. He cheered up everyone, all in a far better state of health than him. I am delighted to report that Tony got his transplant in a successful operation performed by Mr Yacoub. He has gone home and at the time of writing he is doing well, bless him.

'Alf', a bus driver from Liverpool—chirpy, amusing, like most Liverpudlians—was crippled with chronic angina, major blockages of the arteries. He would climb out of bed and try to reach the bathroom. Within minutes he would gasp for breath and collapse with severe pains in his chest. Sitting up seemed to help so he squatted, bent double, on his bed, praying for the pains to go away. I learnt a lot from 'Alf' and that's because he made me feel really ashamed of myself.

Before my heart attack I held a private pilot's licence which entitled me to fly small single-engined aeroplanes. For me it was only a hobby, providing some relaxation, a few thrills, and the fun of exploring the countryside near my home from the air. When I had my heart attack the Civil Aviation Authority suspended my medical certificate and grounded me. It was a severe disappointment. I had taken a year to qualify as a pilot and it seemed that all the effort was for nothing.

One afternoon I talked to 'Alf' about this, moaning about my rotten luck. He looked up at me and said, 'I wouldn't worry about that, Bernard. I'm a bus driver. I love it and I've just lost my job (HGV licences are suspended after a heart attack). In Liverpool there's such bad unemployment I don't stand a chance of getting anything else. I'm on the scrap heap and I'm only 42.'

I felt awful. There was I feeling sorry for myself for losing a hobby, when this man's entire life had been changed. He faced all the anxiety of being a breadwinner without work and he'd lost a job that he really enjoyed.

As a postscript 'Alf' had open heart bypass surgery. He made a rapid and full recovery. As for the job, well I do not know if he will ever drive a bus again.

The whole ward was full of 'characters', the most remarkable being a giant bear of a man who was a professional bouncer by trade. There are problems if you're a bouncer with a heart complaint and have to spend your working life chucking out drunks from a club. 'George' was in hospital to have a pacemaker fitted. I asked 'George' whether he was worried that getting into fights could be damaging to his heart. 'There's noffin' wrong wif me fists, mate,' he said in a cockney accent. 'And I always kick 'em in the goolies before they get anywhere near.'

'George' went home, he's in excellent health, and doubtless still 'kicking 'em in the goolies', dodgy heart or not.

A final surprise during my stay in hospital was that the age of the patients recovering from heart attacks was far younger than I ever expected, in some wards the average was 44. Heart disease is not confined to the elderly. It hits every age and over the years those affected have been getting younger. There were youngsters there, a number of young men in their twenties and the wards were packed with thirty- and forty-year-old cardiac patients either waiting for major surgery or recovering from it.

The Twentieth-Century Disease hits all age groups which is why, as a nation, we must make fighting it a major national priority.

As for me, well my angiogram was done. It was relatively painless except for a huge bruise in the groin where they put in the probe. I returned home to rest for a couple of days eagerly awaiting its results and those of a blood test which would show the level of cholesterol. All would depend on the general condition of my heart. If in a good state then I could begin a new lifestyle in earnest. Ahead I could plan for a life with a healthy diet, lots of exercise and the relief from excessive stress.

Fortunately five months after my heart attack I was still feeling good and praying that my luck would last.

DR ROGER BLACKWOOD

Outpatients appointment

First let me deal with the relevance of Bernard's appointment as an outpatient. This is usually six weeks after the heart attack and is an important time for assessing the future, so crucial that few patients fail to remember to turn up.

If you have any reason to doubt whether you had a heart attack don't hesitate to ask at this visit. There are circumstances where the pain may have been only severe angina and it is important to know.

At this outpatient appointment the doctor will ask questions and examine you to establish whether you have experienced any chest pains, breathlessness caused by heart failure or an abnormal rhythm of the heart, usually occurring as palpitations or lightheadedness. He will also talk to you about the risk factors of heart disease to try to prevent you having another attack.

Bearing in mind that every individual's diagnosis is different, let us examine what you might learn from this outpatient's visit and look at the medical reasons why the tests are conducted. First the potential complaints. If any of these apply to you then do not feel concerned. They are medical problems and there are practical solutions to all of them.

Angina

Angina is produced by the narrowing of a blood vessel. A heart attack is the blockage of a blood vessel so a heart attack itself cannot cause angina. After a heart attack however, another blood vessel may be narrowed and precipitate angina. Angina occurs when the heart is working too hard.

The narrowed blood vessel restricts the flow of blood into the heart muscle so that when the heart is beating harder and faster there is an inadequate amount of blood available. This means an imbalance of supply and demand. If the blood vessels are constricted, you will experience pain in your heart and breathlessness.

If these symptoms develop after a heart attack it is important to report them to your own doctor or consultant. The presence of angina after a heart attack increases the risk of another heart attack, so treatment should start immediately. This can be medical or surgical. It is usual to start with tablets—Beta-Blockers, calcium antagonists or nitrates or a combination of all these. The Beta-Blockers reduce the work-load of the heart so that it requires less blood, and the calcium antagonists work

in a different way but have the same effect. The nitrates open
up blood vessels to flow more freely in the circulation. In
Bernard's case I prescribed Beta-Blockers as a precaution.

Bypass surgery and angioplasty

In many cases tablets will solve the problem but, if for any
reason the angina is not controlled, an operation may be
suggested. This is the coronary artery bypass operation which
has become extremely popular in recent years. The principle
of the operation is to by-pass the narrowed artery with a piece
of vein from your leg and so restore blood flow.

The vein is taken from the surface of a leg and sewn on to
the aorta, the major blood vessel in the body. This operation
is tried and tested surgery, carrying a risk of 1 per cent of
death during surgery. But it has a 90 per cent chance of
the patient being virtually free of pain afterwards. In certain
patients it is also likely to make them live longer.

The operation means staying in hospital for up to ten days
and complete rest for about eight to ten weeks before returning
to work. Generally speaking it can be regarded as a very good
operation.

An alternative is called angioplasty. A tiny balloon is inflated
in the artery at the site of the narrowing and literally squashes
the atheroma out of the way and opens up the blood vessel.
This cannot always be done because many narrowings are
difficult to get at. When it can be done it saves an operation
and means a hospital stay of only a few days.

Heart failure

Breathlessness is caused by heart failure because the heart
muscle fails to pump enough blood around the body and in
particular the lungs. It is easy to imagine that if part of the
heart muscle isn't working the pump becomes inefficient.
Drugs can help the good part of the heart to beat more strongly.
Diuretics take extra fluid away from the heart and so reduce
its work-load. Digoxin is like a heart tonic. It makes the muscle
beat more vigorously.

I prescribed a diuretic for Bernard as well as the Beta-Blockers.

By and large pills work extremely effectively and in most cases easily control any heart failure.

Occasionally the amount of dead muscle is so large that whatever drugs are given, heart failure continues. It is possible to consider an operation. All you do is 'chop out' the dead muscle so that it doesn't interfere with the good muscle.

This is a very good operation in certain circumstances, but it is not possible on a routine basis.

Ultimately if all else fails one might consider a heart transplant. Because there are so few hearts available, this is restricted to young people. But heart transplants do carry an excellent chance of prolonging the patient's life for many years.

Abnormal rhythms

The irritation caused by a heart attack can set up a variety of unusually fast rhythms which can make you feel quite unwell. If allowed to continue unchecked these rhythms can have serious consequences, so if you do experience palpitations or fluttering it must be checked. A lot of palpitations are in fact quite benign and can be detected with a simple ECG recording. In many cases however, it is difficult to catch what is happening and you may need more sophisticated investigation.

Most abnormal rhythms occur without warning and may last from a few moments to a few hours. Even when the symptoms last a long time it is not always easy to get to the doctor's or to a casualty department to get a recording made.

One of the best ways to obtain a recording is to use a twenty-four-hour ECG tape-recording machine. This is done by putting four sticky pads on the chest. Each pad is connected by a wire to a recorder attached to the waistband. The recorder is the size of a personal stereo and uses the same sort of tapes. The tape turns extremely slowly and runs for twenty-four hours, thus hopefully catching the abnormal rhythm. The tape is then put through an analyser which reveals the precise nature of the abnormal rhythm. An alternative method is to give a patient a recorder which he can clip on if he suffers an attack.

Once the rhythm has been detected the appropriate tablets

can be prescribed. There are a variety of drugs which can be used which allow almost every palpitation to be treated successfully.

Exercise test

Bernard has described his own visit to the National Heart Hospital and during this he had an exercise test. The purpose of this is to find out how your heart behaves under stress. We call it a Treadmill Test. The object of the test is not to see how fast a person can go before he drops off the back but to raise the heart rate from a resting level of 70–80 beats per minute up to 140–150. At this rate, usually reached in five to seven minutes, the ECG of a heart will reveal any underlying abnormalities. A consultant might then prescribe some tablets if he sees ECG changes.

Risk factors

Then, as in Bernard's case the consultant cardiologist will spell out the various risk factors which you can avoid to prevent the same problems with the heart happening again. The consultant will mention smoking, high blood pressure and blood fats. Smoking in particular is the one thing you must not do. Stopping smoking reduces the risk of another heart attack by 50 per cent over five years. Reducing high blood pressure and high fats certainly reduces the risk of further heart attacks but these factors are not so significant as before the first attack.

Losing weight can help particularly if you are 30 per cent over your ideal weight and there is good evidence that all these factors together may add up to your benefit if they are all reduced. In Bernard's case he needs to stop smoking, reduce the fat content in his diet, reduce weight by about one and a half to two stone and embark on a carefully monitored and structured exercise programme.

It is very difficult to know if stress is an important factor at this stage, but one rather curious advantage of a heart attack is that it may make you take a step back from your life and help you decide what your priorities are. Many people climb a somewhat mythical ladder in their careers not really sure of what they are aiming for. As I have said earlier, some will rush to work before all the others and come home later; but to impress whom? There is a feeling that if you rush around at work looking busy and full of energy you will be promoted. Is this really the case?

There are four aspects which should be considered at this stage.

Ambition

If you want to be chairman of a huge company or the Prime Minister that's fine so long as you accept the stresses and strains. However, many people do not and, when they look at themselves, their partner and their children, they may decide that where they have got to is actually sufficient. Almost every ambitious person denies any ambition so it may take a little discussion with your nearest and dearest to find out what you are really like.

Stress

You must sort out what is good and bad stress in your life. We all work better and feel most satisfied at the end of the day if we have had a little stress, as long as we enjoyed it. You may enjoy flying abroad, chairing a meeting or writing an article and that can be classed as acceptable stress. However bad stress is that which irritates you; it may be a colleague at work or travelling one and a half hours to the office each day and so on. It is not easy to work all this out and many take six months to establish a routine which is sensible. The object is to get rid of the bad stress, if at all possible.

Holidays

It is wise to take holidays. Many people may take one day here and another there. It is difficult to wind down in less than a week. So a fortnight or, if you are lucky, three weeks is ideal.

Hobbies

Try to develop a hobby if you do not have one. It does not have to be a sport but any activity to divert the mind away from the normal stresses of daily life. Also get down to it immediately rather than put off the idea of starting a hobby until next week or next month.

Aspirin

Although your doctor may give you tablets to take there has been a lot in the newspapers about taking an aspirin a day. It appears that a single junior aspirin (75 milligrams a day) may reduce the substance called thromboxanes which tends to make blood clot and blood vessels contract. Also it may increase other substances called prostacyclins which have the reverse effect. Trials on this showed that there was a reduction of between 15 and 30 per cent in the death rate among those taking aspirin. Since aspirin is almost harmless and very few people have side-effects it is perfectly reasonable to take a junior aspirin a day.

For the future

'The road to hell is paved with good intentions' and this is particularly significant during the rehabilitation after a heart attack. Many set out to change their lives and become healthy but gradually slip back to their old habits of smoking, working excessively and eating dripping toast and fried bread.

If you are aware of this problem it is less likely to happen, but it does justify the circumstances of the nagging wife who actually may love you enough to want to keep you alive. As for Bernard, well, he 'survived' the exercise test and the angiogram. Indeed his tests were extremely favourable and I shall analyse what was wrong with him in Chapter 12. It looks as though the lad is going to survive but for how long almost totally depends on him.

11. Chips with everything

BERNARD FALK

I have always loved eating. From a very early age I learned that food was not only enjoyable but that it kept me going too. Sadly I have always eaten the wrong sort of food. My favourite meal for breakfast is bacon and eggs, tomatoes, buttered toast, coffee and cream. I adore steak and chips for lunch and there's nothing like a big steaming hot curry and rice for dinner particularly when you are bombed out of your head from downing too many Scotches down at the Dog and Duck. This shouldn't rule out the occasional snack in between meals, like a chocolate biscuit midday or a sandwich at teatime.

Now you know why I've always been a bit overweight. All right then, a lot overweight. In reality I stand 5 ft 9 ins tall in my socks, with the holes in the toes, and I weigh 13 stone 8 lbs (8 lbs less than when I suffered my heart attack). This means I am about two stone above the proper weight for my height.

But I have embarked on a steady reduction in the amount of saturated fat I eat. This stuff sounds disgusting and it plays merry hell with your heart. Indeed dairy products are wonderful to eat but rotten for hearts. And while that may not sound very scientific I am not trying to play the expert.

I have learned about healthier eating from Angela Cristofoli. She is a community dietician, a member of the Dietetic Department of the East Berks Health Authority and works largely outside a hospital environment in schools, health centres, factories, offices and with the general public. Her objective is to encourage people to adopt healthier eating. So, I asked her, how can we protect ourselves from our own ignorance about food and diet?

ANGELA CRISTOFOLI

As a nation we eat far too much fat and, in particular, saturated fats. These come mainly from animal products as opposed to vegetables, and cereal foods. We could get most of our energy from staple foods like bread, cereals, potatoes and pulses and cut down on animal foods.

Typical foods with a large amount of saturated fats in them are fried meals, red meat, vegetables soaked in butter, high fat puddings, anything with cream. You might think that a lean steak is all right but it can still be 10 per cent fat. Meat pies, sausages and bacon can be quite fatty, cheese as well, which is why doctors and dieticians recommend you eat more low fat cheeses rather than a large chunk of Cheddar.

So why do we eat these foods? Largely because of their availability and we are all victims of aggressive advertising by the food manufacturers. Also to be fair, they taste nice. Fat helps to make foods more palatable.

The body needs a certain amount of fat. It provides vitamins A, D & E and essential fatty acids, but over the years we have gradually increased our intake of saturated fats. This is because we have become more reliant on meat products, convenience and ready made foods, rather than natural things like cereals, vegetables and fruits.

The concentration of fat-like substances in the blood stream, one of which is cholesterol (made from saturated fats), is an important factor in the rapid and horrific growth of heart disease in the western world, although Mediterranean countries like Italy seem to have a lower incidence of heart disease, probably because they use olive oil as opposed to butter or animal fats like lard. Of course olive oil is expensive in the UK but cooking oils with polyunsaturated fats are easily available, like sunflower, corn or soya oils and special soft margarines. Also high in polyunsaturates are nuts and oily fish such as herring, mackerel and trout.

Taking your diet more seriously is vital if we are to cut down on the death rate due to heart attacks. Remember that at present one in four people will develop heart disease, so every family is likely to have someone affected.

There are several golden rules which do not mean a drastic

alteration to your diet. It will mean *moderating* the *total* amount of fat you eat and *cutting down* on these *saturated* animal fats. It does *not* mean you can never enjoy a nice steak again or a bag of chips or bacon and eggs for breakfast. It *does* mean reducing the number of times you eat them.

The object is to persuade your taste buds to become less reliant on foods which, if consumed in large quantities over the years, can do you harm and lead to a heart attack.

An excellent booklet issued free by the Health Education Council called *Guide to Healthy Eating* is an easy guide on how you can moderate your diet. Many local authorities have booklets on healthy eating like the East Berkshire Health Authority with its Health Promotion and Dietetic units.

Here are some tips on how to reduce your fat intake.

Cooking

First avoid frying food. Grill, poach or bake it instead. Try not to add extra fat to meat and vegetables. You do not need a knob of butter in your baked potato. Try a little cottage cheese, chives, natural yoghurt or baked beans instead. This is delicious and healthier.

Casseroling or stewing is an excellent way of cooking meat and you can use cheaper cuts. But remember to spoon off any fat that comes to the surface and this is best done when the casserole cools. And cut off any visible fat before you start.

Also drain fat from curries and gravy. Avoid cooking in lard, hard margarine, butter and ghee. Mixed vegetable oils which have lots of saturated fat need to be avoided too. Instead try using a non-stick pan, grilling food, or find some lower fat recipes.

Meat

Eat less red meat. Use more chicken, fish and turkey. The fat in chicken and turkey is in the skin, so simply remove the skin. Fish is an excellent food particularly oily fish like mackerel, herrings and trout but *do not cook the fish in batter, deep-fried in fat*. It totally defeats the purpose. Try baking or even barbecuing your fish in the summer. Rub a few herbs over the fish, perhaps a little wine, a sliver of soft margarine, bake or barbecue and the results will be delicious. You can serve this with new boiled potatoes sprinkled with mint or parsley, and a fresh salad.

Milk

Use skimmed or semi-skimmed milk as opposed to silver top or full-cream milk. Skimmed milk is very low in fat and has the same protein and calcium as ordinary milk. However, this does not apply to children under five. There is some evidence that they should have full-cream milk during these important formative years.

Say NO to cream. Try natural yoghurt instead. If you can't live without cream on your strawberries then use single cream rather than double. Remember that condensed and evaporated milk contain a lot of fat so use them as little as possible.

Butter and Margarine

Use less of both and try to wean your palate towards the low fat spreads. This does not mean you can never taste butter again. Just be careful how much you use. Remember that low fat spreads and soft margarine spread far more easily than butter so you don't have the trouble of melting them down when straight out of the fridge.

Whatever fat you use, both margarine and butter are high in calories, and can lead to being overweight, so use them sparingly.

Cheese

Try to check your cheese for its fat content. I'm afraid it might seem a little unpatriotic but most of the English cheeses like Stilton and our biggest selling Cheddar have a high saturation fat content. For example 60 grams of cottage cheese contains 2 grams of fat. The same amount of Stilton contains 22 grams of fat. Which is better for you? But if you cannot live without your Cheddar or Stilton then have a little once a week as a treat. You will look forward to it and consequently enjoy it all the more, or use a strong flavoured cheese (especially in cooking) so that you use less of it.

By and large harder cheeses are less good for your cholesterol levels than the lower fat cheeses and varieties like cottage cheese are tasty with many variations nowadays and excellent for your health. Edam, Brie, Camembert, low fat curd/cream cheese also have less fat.

Eggs

These have been much maligned in recent years with concerns about their cholesterol content but new evidence has been emerging that says eggs are probably not so bad for us as first thought. Maybe it's the way we tend to cook eggs in this country, *fried* instead of poached or scrambled with lots of *butter* and *milk*. What we should try to do is cut down the number of eggs we eat to about six a week. That isn't a big sacrifice is it?

Fibre, fruit and vegetables

Healthy eating doesn't mean eating less of everything—you can eat *more* fibre. If you eat vegetable- and cereal-based dishes you can eat considerably more and feel less hungry than if your diet is dominated by dairy products and red meat. Use boiled or baked potatoes instead of chips, try brown rice instead of white which contains much starch and less fibre, wholemeal pasta, and wholemeal bread. Incidentally eat the skins of baked potatoes. And eat more pulse vegetables like beans and peas, even baked beans. You do not need to add extra bran to your diet; concentrate instead on increasing your intake of the natural high fibre foods.

You should eat plenty of fruit and the varieties available in the shops today make for exciting and varied éating. Even soft fruits like melons or oranges contain fibre and because fruit and vegetables contain a lot of water they are low in calories and help you stay slim.

In all, fibre is the single most important form of food likely to be lacking at present in the everyday diet of people living in the western world.

Sugar and salt

Most reports do not relate sugar and salt to heart disease although excessive salt can cause high blood pressure so we should try to reduce our intake.

In Britain on average we buy almost a pound of packet sugar per person per week and we eat nearly twice as much when you count all the sugars added to processed food such as sweets, soft drinks, cakes, jam and a lot of savoury foods. The problem with sugar is that apart from the damage it does to your teeth, it tends to make you fat. Cutting back on sugar is the easiest way to cut calories without losing any nutrients. And staying slim or your proper weight for your height and build reduces the heart's work-load. Our sodium intake is high, and this comes from salt we add to foods as well as manufactured foods, e.g. cured meats, bottled sauces, salted snack foods.

Rather than giving up salt and sugar altogether which can ruin people's enjoyment of what they eat and drink I recommend that people try to cut them down gradually. It is better eventually to get used to foods that are less sweet or salty and this comes over a gradual period. It is even better to reduce your sugar intake from two teaspoons in a cup of tea to half a teaspoon and eventually you will be less dependent on sugar. The same applies to salt. A gradual decrease is often more effective than stopping altogether and then longing for what you are missing.

Alcohol

Alcohol in small amounts may be beneficial when it comes to heart patients. In large quantities it acts like a poison and damages the liver. The problem with alcohol is that it is full of calories, so heavy that even moderate drinkers can put on weight particularly if they eat too much as well.

To keep within a safe limit men should not drink more than 6 standard* drinks or their equivalent two or three times a week, and women should not drink more than 2 or 3 standard drinks two or three times a week.

* A standard drink is ½ pint beer or single measure of spirits or 1 glass wine.

The problem with Bernard of course is that he has always eaten a bit too much and he was brought up on the wrong sorts of foods, chips with everything, fried meals rather than grilled or poached. He loves red meat and has always eaten very little fish. His own commentary shows his great enthusiasm for alcohol. I only hope he heeds the warnings.

Remember that eating healthier food does not mean abandoning all the things you like. A gradual reduction in the less healthy foods is more sensible. Moderation is the key word and I promise you will feel better too.

12. For the technical
or those who can pronounce the names

MEDICAL REPORT

Re: Bernard Falk born 16:2:43

20th October 1986

This 43-year-old man was seen by me in the outpatient clinic. He was apparently well until the end of April 1986 when he complained of chest pain. He was admitted at the end of May with an acute myocardial infarction sited anteriorly. He used to be a very heavy smoker and has a family history of ischaemic heart disease.

He has made an excellent recovery and by the time I saw him in July of this year he did not have evidence of myocardial ischaemia and his exercise test was negative to Stage 3 of exercise. He did not complain of chest pain.

In view of his young age angiography was performed. This showed his left ventricular function to be good and the extent of the infarction to be small.

There is a stenosis of the left anterior descending coronary artery which is presumably the infarct vessel. The remainder of the coronary tree shows no significant obstruction.

This patient has made an excellent recovery from his acute myocardial infarction and on the basis of the exercise test and angiographic findings he has an excellent prognosis. He has stopped smoking and is losing weight. He does have evidence of a Type IIB hypercholesterolaemia and is modifying his diet accordingly.

Kim Fox
Consultant Cardiologist

BERNARD FALK

I am convinced that doctors use language that no one else can understand simply to confuse their patients. That letter is about me but what on earth does it mean? Am I knackered or not?

Of course once we ordinary folks actually learn to understand this strange medical language then it strips away the mystique which doctors jealously guard for themselves. Maybe we might look upon the guys in the white coats as human. Human, with weaknesses too, which is what they're really worried about.

I am only kidding. Kim Fox is a highly respected cardiologist and with Roger he has been looking after me with superlative expertise, care, patience and a lot of kindness. I have to say that in case they let me die.

However we really need a translation into plain language.

DR ROGER BLACKWOOD

For ordinary folks: A translation

Bernard Falk was admitted to hospital with a heart attack affecting the front part of his heart. He used to be a very heavy smoker and his father died of a heart attack. He has made an excellent recovery and by the time I saw him in July he had no evidence of heart strain and his exercise test was completely normal up to walking 3 m.p.h. up a 1 in 8 slope. Whilst walking at this speed he did not suffer any chest pains.

Because he was so young, we tested him, using dye squirted into his coronary arteries under X-ray control.

His heart was beating vigorously and the area of damage was seen to be small. There was a narrowing of one of his major blood vessels at the front of his heart just above where the heart attack had occurred. The other blood vessels were basically normal.

This patient has made an excellent recovery from his sudden heart attack and on the basis of the tests performed on him he has an excellent chance of living a normal lifespan. He has stopped smoking and has lost weight. His blood cholesterol is slightly raised as are his other fats so he is already eating a low fat and high fibre diet.

BERNARD FALK

Thank you very much, Dr Fox and Roger. So now I know. Stop smoking, eat less fat, and more high fibre food, lose weight, and I should live a normal lifespan.

13. The patient and the doctor

There are many questions left unanswered for the person who might feel that their lifestyle runs the risk of their suffering a heart attack, for those who have experienced one already and of course for the families involved. Heart disease has such a profound effect on the populations of the world particularly in the so-called 'developed' countries. If we are to fight this mass killer it is important to increase the awareness of everyone, particularly the general public, on the causes, the prevention and the recovery. In this we bring the patient, Bernard Falk, and the cardiologist, Roger Blackwood, together. It is question time between the ignorant and the informed and although it repeats much of the substance of this book we hope it will clarify some of the main issues and deal with some we have not touched. Bernard has selected his Top 50 questions for Roger to answer.

1. Why are some people more prone to heart disease than others?

We don't know. Much of what happens to us is predestined from birth. Some people are just born with the tendency to have heart disease. Indeed there is no way we could stop everyone having heart attacks by just cutting out smoking. Susceptible people may have a greater tendency to clotting of their blood as well as being more prone to narrowing of the arteries.

2. What are the major risk factors that are preventable?

The major preventable risk factor is an inappropriate diet with smoking and high blood pressure close behind. Then come stress, lack of exercise and obesity. Combinations of these risk factors in certain people multiply the risk considerably.

3. If you have been a heavy smoker and then give it up, is it possible to undo any damage you may have done to your health?

Yes. In the first year your risk of a heart attack is 50 per cent less. In succeeding years the risk grows ever nearer to normal.

4. What causes high blood pressure?

We haven't a clue. For many years the theory has been that if we consume too much salt, starting in childhood, we may end up with high blood pressure. If the body is overloaded with salt, water is retained and the amount of blood in the body is increased. If this is more blood to pump around then up goes the blood pressure. However, as yet, there is no proof of this. It is true that in a tiny percentage of patients, about ½ per cent, a cause is found which is permanently treatable. These cases usually occur in younger people. An example of this is a tumour which produces excessive adrenalin. The tumour can be removed with subsequent cure of high blood pressure.

5. What steps can be taken to reduce the dangers created by high blood pressure?

You can help your own blood pressure by losing weight, drinking less alcohol, stopping smoking, reducing salt, and taking more exercise. This will reduce your blood pressure by 5 to 10 per cent, taking you from having mildly high blood pressure into the normal range. However, the majority of people cannot manage these simple measures, and pressures are often too high for anything other than tablets. If tablets reduce your blood pressure to normal then your risk is back to normal.

6. Are some people more prone to high blood pressure than others and is age an influencing factor?

High blood pressure does tend to run in families, although it is not automatic that you will get high blood pressure if your parents had it. You are not more prone to high blood pressure if you are living a stressful life. The technical term is hypertension which suggests it is all related to stress. This is not true at all. If you consume excessive salt you are probably more likely to develop high blood pressure but absolute proof is not available. Blood pressure does rise gradually with age so the level at which treatment is required is significantly higher in the elderly.

7. How do we assess whether our diet is healthy or not?
Your diet should contain less animal fat and more fibre. It is not a sin to eat dairy products but in general we eat too much of them. Fibre, such as vegetables and bran, should be eaten in a sensible quantity.

8. Should parents feel guilty if they feed their children with traditional foods, like bacon-and-egg breakfast?
Yes, to a certain extent. We know that fatty streaks appear in the arteries of children as young as three years old. So a high fat diet can start to cause trouble at that age. Secondly children will tend to consider those foods as the 'norm' and this will condition their eating habits in later life. It is in the formative years that we develop our life-long habits.

9. Is the growth of convenience foods influencing the rise in heart attacks?
There is no evidence for this but the idea of 'chips' (and so salt) with everything is far from ideal.

10. Is stress a factor in heart attacks?
Evidence suggests it is not a major factor in itself. But stress can lead to excessive drinking, smoking and lack of exercise. It is difficult to measure stress so it is hard to evaluate it fully as a major factor.

11. How can we reduce stress in our lives?
There are numerous books on how to relax, stress-less tapes and people to teach you how to relax. Find the best way for you as an individual. Start by talking to your doctor about it.

12. What effect does exercise have on heart attacks?
People who sit around all day are somewhat more prone to heart attacks than those who take vigorous exercise. But even active marathon runners can have a heart attack. Sensible exercise is good commonsense and in turn may lead to stopping smoking and a better diet. You cannot pretend that if you play squash three times a week you can smoke forty cigarettes a day and get away with it.

13. Is exercise wise for a patient recovering from a heart attack?
Yes. The heart recovers its original physical shape more

quickly if you exercise, and psychologically it is of enormous value.

14. How does a cardiac patient find out what sort of exercise to take?

Ask the doctor. No two coronaries are identical and before embarking on any exercise you must take professional advice. Once you have learned to take your own pulse, you can exercise up to a heart rate of 120.

15. Will jogging prevent heart attacks?

No. As exercise it will help but it certainly is no guarantee of prevention. In addition some people drop dead whilst jogging so see your doctor before you suddenly take it up after years of abstinence. Start with a very short distance and increase this gradually. Most authorities recommend twenty minutes of modest exercise, a brisk walk, gentle jogging, and swimming. And you should do this about three times a week. Also try walking up a staircase instead of taking the lift, park the car half a mile away and walk to the office and do a few simple exercises each day.

16. Is heart disease largely confined to the affluent or the middle classes?

It is not confined to any class but the pattern is changing. The so-called 'middle class' have become more health-conscious and consequently they are suffering fewer heart attacks than manual workers.

17. What influence does alcohol have on heart attacks?

It can raise the blood fats and these can narrow arteries. Excessive alcohol can make the heart very flabby which puts you at risk if you have a coronary. In addition alcohol raises the blood pressure in susceptible people.

18. Why are men more prone to attack than women?

Probably hormones. Unfortunately we can't test this as men are unwilling to take female hormones which would make them impotent.

19. Why has there been an increase in the number of women having heart attacks?

It may be the increase in smoking, so many work outside

the home and suffer greater stress in their daily lives, and the contraceptive pill appears to be a significant factor. However, it is rare to see a non-smoking woman having a coronary before the menopause.

20. Are some nationalities more vulnerable than others?

Caucasians (whites) are twice as prone as non-whites. The Japanese seem to be less prone even when they eat a western diet. We do not know why.

21. Why is Britain becoming the heart attack capital of the world?

Apathy. In this country we don't seem interested in health. We make an enormous fuss of meningitis which accounts for about 100 deaths a year in this country. Heart attacks are not taken so seriously, probably because to combat the disease we have to change our private lifestyles. Rather than face up to the truth we ignore it.

22. Why don't we do something about it?

We all think it's someone else's job to look after our health. We are protected by the National Health Service and never fear the huge medical bills which can cripple families in places like America. This discourages us from having regular medical screening which would avoid problems before they occur.

23. Where can I find out more information on preventing heart attacks and what to do after someone has had one? What leaflets or books are available?

Your own doctor's surgery will have plenty of information, and many bookshops have a variety of books which you can purchase. The British Heart Foundation is always willing to help, often free of charge. Their address is: British Heart Foundation, 102 Gloucester Place, London, W1H 4DH.

24. What community schemes can be adopted in order to fight heart disease?

Education programmes on a personal scale are probably the most appropriate although there will always be people who ignore advice. I think that community schemes like the Slough Health Habit (see Appendix) have the best chance of success. The Government has started 'Heartbeat Wales' and is due to begin a major programme on a national scale and there are some excellent community exercise programmes run by doctors in places like Manchester and Preston.

25. What are Bernard's chances of living to an old age?

Very good, as long as he doesn't start smoking again and returning to his bad habits. His heart is in very good shape now and he must take the full responsibility for keeping it that way.

26. After a heart attack why is it that some patients recover and others have another attack relatively soon after?

No two hearts are the same. That is why we look at people carefully after a heart attack. Some may need an operation. With the best medicine in the world some people are going to end up with complications.

This is particularly true of those who carry on smoking, refuse to take their tablets which they have been prescribed, ignore their diets and generally continue to abuse themselves. The individual must make an effort as well as the doctor.

27. With my diagnosed condition do I have to worry about dropping dead every time I feel a pain in the chest?

No. People can have curious pains in the chest after a heart attack. This is usually due to spasm of muscles between the ribs. Some people may get angina. If they get a pain it is a warning sign, so slow down what you are doing at the time. It is a defence mechanism of the body, not a sign of damage or impending doom.

28. If we are with someone who has the symptoms of a heart attack what should we do?

Stay calm, call a doctor or 999. Stay with the patient and speak casually and gently to him. If you get frightened so will he and the pain will get worse. The majority of patients will be fine until the doctor or ambulancemen arrive. Occasionally you may witness someone having a cardiac arrest. There is a major campaign under way to teach people the basics of resuscitation and you could save a life by finding out about it.

29. How important is an annual check-up with your doctor?

It is all part of bothering about your health and screening can show up problems before they become serious. Extremely important in relation to the heart is the need to check your blood pressure.

30. What will happen to a patient at an annual medical?

The number of tests we can do on the human body is infinite but most 'medicals' will be straightforward questions and examining you by palpation and a stethoscope. Apart from commonsense things like your weight, the doctor will take your pulse and blood pressure, check your urine for sugar and listen to your heart and chest. He will discourage you from smoking and perhaps arrange for an ECG or chest X-ray. It is very civilised and painless. If your doctor is unable to do it —and he gets no payment—you can go privately. This is expensive, £150 or so. However that does include blood tests, an ECG, ear tests, breathing tests and eye tests.

31. Is it better to seek preventive medicine privately or can the NHS cope?

The NHS couldn't cope if everyone wanted an annual medical tomorrow. Doctors' practices are very stretched. Most GPs do two surgeries per day with about 50 patients to see, plus visits. It may leave them with two hours per day to do 'medicals'. Each medical would take at least half an hour, so in a year he might get through about 800 annual check-ups out of his list of 3,000 plus. It just doesn't fit in. If there's an emergency then this stretches the doctor even further. We cannot get away from the fact that preventive medicine will cost money but it is no surprise that those who can afford it go privately.

32. How do you take your own pulse rate and what is the significance of this?

When you are sitting down quietly your pulse is about 70/min. When you walk it goes up to 110/min. When you run it may go up to 150/min. One Grand Prix racing driver patient of mine reached 210/min at Le Mans. If you are a fairly sedentary character it is best to keep your pulse below about 120/min, until you get fit. This is very important after a heart attack or heart operation.

You take your pulse at the wrist over what is called the radial artery. With palm facing upwards feel with your fingers about 1 cm in from the thumb side of your hand, about 2½ cm above your wrist bones.

33. Should a person take his own blood pressure? Domestic machines are available so are they worth the money?

Purchase a blood pressure machine if you wish. If you are a born worrier then do not buy one. Blood pressure is a continuous variable and one single recording is almost meaningless. If your blood pressure is persistently raised then this is cause for concern but nothing to panic about. The problem is that some of these electronic machines produce spurious results every now and then. Take your blood pressure again, several times if necessary.

34. What medical advances are being made to combat heart disease?

Artificial hearts, improved surgical techniques, laser treatment of narrowed coronary arteries, drugs to dissolve clots, nuclear magnetic resonance scanning and histrochemical techniques are just a few exciting advances.

35. What is a bypass operation and how successful is it?

Rather as a bypass goes round the bottleneck of the village, the heart bypass operation is when a piece of vein bypasses the narrowing of a coronary artery. It is a plumbing operation restoring blood flow to the part of an artery beyond the blockage. Although enormous skill is required it is not a complicated operation. A superficial vein is taken from the patient's leg and up to five bypasses are inserted into the heart. This operation relieves pain totally or almost totally in 90 per cent of patients with angina and overall carries a 1 per cent risk of death. Therefore it is a very good operation indeed.

36. After a heart attack how long should a patient take to recover before returning to work?

A heart attack heals just like a broken leg in about six weeks. At that point there is no reason why you shouldn't be going back to work albeit part-time for the first two weeks. If your job is manual you may need longer. Always ask your doctor before you go back to work.

37. Do patients recovering from a heart attack suffer any psychological problems, particularly in matters of confidence?

Yes. A heart heals much faster than the brain. It is a mixture of fear, desperation, frustration and anger about what has happened with the subsequent feeling of inadequacy. Reassurance and love from the patient's family is terribly important. Time heals these problems but they are sometimes crippling. No one should end up a cardiac cripple, but with the best medicine in the world it still happens.

38. What can a family do to help if a patient becomes bad-tempered or irritable?

Be understanding. A heart attack with its attendant psychological reaction leads people to depression, fatigue and irritability. You must do your best to support the person concerned through this difficult time.

39. Can a damaged heart recover sufficiently to allow a patient a long and active life?

Yes, absolutely. In the majority of cases it would be difficult to see the heart attack with the naked eye if we were to look at the heart directly. The healing process is quite remarkable, leaving only an insignificant scar. Quite a number of people die in old age and are found by chance to have had a coronary years before without themselves ever having known it.

40. Why is the age of heart attack victims getting younger?

The only explanation for this has been an increase in the risk factors, particularly diet, over the last fifty years. However it is a fact so we should make a lot more effort than we do.

41. Are people in certain jobs more prone to heart attacks than others?

There was a time when it was thought that people 'at the top' were more prone to heart attacks. It now appears more likely to be those who are frustrated in jobs where their initiative is stifled. The so-called 'middle management' person with a boss who frustrates a career or progress. Bottled up stress is the thing which is really bad.

42. Are you allowed to continue driving after a heart attack?

The recommendation from the DVLC in Swansea is that the patient waits eight weeks before starting to drive again. It may be possible to drive sooner, so ask your doctor. After an uncomplicated heart attack you may be able to drive after four weeks. You should inform your insurance company but if you are fit and well they should not increase your premiums.

43. For the holder of a HGV licence (a lorry or bus driver) does a heart attack mean losing your job?

Unfortunately you will lose your licence if you hold either a Public Service Vehicle licence (PSV) or Heavy Goods Vehicle licence (HGV). This is the law. Getting it back is possible but very complicated and you will have to seek your own doctor's advice and inform the DVLC in Swansea.

44. What effect can a heart attack have on a person's sex life and how soon after can sex resume? Is sex dangerous to a cardiac patient?

Sexual intercourse can begin with the patient's regular partner three or four weeks after a coronary. This is the equivalent of a fifteen-minute walk followed by a flight of stairs (the orgasm). It is very important for men and women to resume sexual intercourse because it boosts their confidence.

If you experience pain or breathlessness walking for fifteen minutes then speak to your doctor before resuming intercourse. Note that we are talking about your regular partner. With a casual partner your orgasm could be like climbing five or six flights of stairs. The strains of casual sex are far greater.

45. After a heart attack is it better to recuperate in hospital or at home?

Any complications resulting from a heart attack are likely to occur in the first forty-eight hours and then rapidly diminish up to seven days. In the majority of cases your doctor will recommend that you go to hospital for a week because it is difficult to know at the outset who is going to have a complication. Your doctor may choose to look after you at home where it is much more restful and only send you to hospital if he suspects an impending complication. The majority of young people are admitted to hospital whilst many older patients will stay at home.

46. What is the average length of stay that a patient should remain in hospital particularly after an operation?

Seven to ten days is the average length. Most patients will be in hospital after both a heart attack and a heart operation. It could be longer of course if there are any complications.

47. After a heart attack should a patient be treated by a general practitioner or seek the regular care of a cardiologist?

Most GPs are more than capable of looking after you when you get home. There are too few cardiologists to go round. It is usual to visit a hospital as an outpatient six weeks or so after your heart attack and unless there are any complications the GPs will continue from there.

48. Are transplants or artificial hearts going to defeat heart disease?

Not a chance. There is probably a maximum of 100 or so heart transplants per year in this country. This will never increase unless we actively run over large numbers of young people. The majority of effective donors are accident victims. There is a long way to go before artificial hearts offer an effective treatment. Prevention, changing people's lifestyles and reducing the risk factors make up the sensible approach.

49. How important are donors and what are the consequences of carrying a donor card in view of public anxiety about doctors taking organs before people are clinically dead?

Donors are vital. So many lives could be saved and problems alleviated by organ donation such as hearts, livers and kidneys. Three of my patients have had heart transplants and the effect upon them is stunning. How much better it would be if some good came from the death of a loved one. It is clearly a dreadful time for the relations of a dying patient but the thought that others might live as a result cannot upset the sensitivity of any decent person. Doctors go to great lengths to make sure that all the formal criteria of death of a patient are checked and nowadays no one should fear this aspect. I only hope that the public lose any anxieties in this area and help many desperate people. If you have ever witnessed a patient slowly dying of heart failure you will know what I mean.

50. What are the prospects of eradicating heart disease altogether?

We will never totally eradicate heart disease and we all have to die sometime. If we could reduce the incidence of heart attacks in this country by 25 per cent as has been done in the United States, there would be as many as 50,000 less deaths a year.

14. How will heart disease be treated in the future?

DR ROGER BLACKWOOD

Heart attacks

Research at present is concentrating on the clotting mechanism which causes the final blockage in the artery. Why are some people more prone? Why does it occur at the narrowed site of the artery? If we can identify what actually happens we might be able to prevent at least some heart attacks.

There are substances which keep arteries open and blood flowing, while another group causes arteries to contract and blood clot. It may be the balance between these two which determines the ultimate clot in a heart attack. Although not based on strong evidence aspirin is thought to influence this balance favourably.

Once the clot has formed it would seem logical to 'unclot' it. We cannot do this surgically without serious risks.

Two drugs have been developed which dissolve clots if you get the chemicals in quickly. This opens up the exciting prospect of offering an actual treatment of a heart attack before any complications occur, although it will be five years before they finish testing these drugs.

Heart failure

Heart transplants captured the public's imagination in 1967 when Professor Christiaan Barnard performed the first operation in Cape Town. There was then a flurry of transplants but the results were disappointing because of the phenomenon of rejection. The recipient's body into which the new heart is placed does not recognise it as part of itself and sees it as foreign in the same way as a virus or bacteria. The body attacks the heart until it gets weaker and weaker and then fails altogether. Then the drug Cyclosporin came along. This counteracted the rejection process so effectively that transplants are now on the increase again because the long-term survival rates are so good. If you ever meet a patient who has had a heart transplant you will know how good the operation is but there will never be enough transplants to 'go around' all those who need one, hence the attempted development of an artificial heart.

Artificial hearts

The problems of developing an ideal artificial heart are very considerable.

First you need a power pack which lasts a long time and at present there is nothing small enough to fit in a chest. It would be difficult to put a car battery in place of one of the lungs. The power source has to be external and at present is rather like dragging a small fridge around with you all the time. Secondly any artificial material in the body, e.g. plastic, tends to promote clotting of the blood and the few artificial heart patients to date have suffered from repeated strokes. Thirdly the cost in money and human time is out of all proportion to its present benefit. There are other technical problems at the moment and their current value is in keeping somebody alive until a transplant becomes available.

New drugs and haemoperfusion

Haemoperfusion is a method like kidney dialysis for taking away excess fluid from the patient who has extreme heart failure, someone for example who is waiting for a heart operation. Only rarely would it be appropriate, but it may also contribute valuable information to our knowledge of the mechanism of heart failure. There is a constant search for new drugs particularly in heart failure. Drugs already available like Captopril have benefited enormous numbers of patients and drugs under investigation like Corwin may have a very bright future in the treatment of heart failure.

Angina

Coronary artery bypass grafting will probably increase in its frequency because the results are so good, but angioplasty is becoming more common. (This is when a 'balloon' is inserted into a narrowed or blocked artery and literally flattens any deposits.) Newer catheters are being developed to achieve access to more complicated narrowings. Because angioplasty does not involve cutting the patient up in any way it has great advantages and we will see more and more of this as time goes by.

Another exciting development is the use of lasers to 'burn away' the narrowings. This process is in its very early stages but successes in animal experiments are very encouraging. However it will be several years before such a technique becomes generally available.

As with heart failure there are even newer drugs coming on to the market for angina, many of which will be very beneficial.

Arrhythmias

These are irregular rhythms produced by an irritable heart and on occasions can be quite serious and disabling. For most occasions drugs solve the problem but many new compounds are becoming available. One advance in this field is the development of machines which will 'catch' an attack.

So many patients have palpitations only once a week that the current methods of recording, like an ECG, normally fail to capture the 'attack'. Machines like the Chiltern Box which a patient can carry around with him for weeks on end if necessary, and then 'clip on' to an arm and leg to make a recording, are very valuable in this field. They are cheap (£400) and record for fifteen minutes.

In the event of drugs being unable to control abnormal heart rhythms sophisticated computer programmable pacemakers may be able to correct electrically both fast and slow heart rates. They are very expensive but fortunately are rarely needed. In addition it is occasionally possible to separate and cut out offending irritable areas of the heart which become the focus of harmful rhythms. This is high-technology surgery because you first have to 'map out' the offending area by taking numerous electrical recordings and then either cut the tracts out with a knife or freeze them.

High blood pressure

The advance in this field is the discovery of chemicals secreted by the heart which rid the body of unwanted salt and appear to be more powerful than anything previously discovered. If we overload the body with salt for years we may end up with high blood pressure. The discovery may have very important implications for treatment by both emphasising salt avoidance and the development of drugs which might correct the system.

Other advances

Investigating the advance of Nuclear Magnetic Resonance has been very exciting. This technique enables one to find out what is going on inside the living cell without the need to stick needles into it or cut it open with a knife. You can literally 'see' into organs like the heart and not only observe the structure very accurately indeed but also discover how healthy it is. The machines are terribly expensive (between half and a million pounds) but are likely to provide a huge leap in research knowledge of the heart as well as other organs.

Perhaps the biggest field of change is in the development of new drugs, like those which lower blood fats. Alas there are no instant slimming drugs. Anyone who claims that is an impostor. Drugs can be used temporarily to reduce your appetite but should not be used permanently. A number of operations are available whereby your bowel can be operated upon to avoid absorbing the food you eat. However they do have some drawbacks and are not generally available.

There will certainly be many more advances in cardiology in the next decade in investigation, treatment and basic research. The prospects are very exciting indeed.

15. Conclusion

BERNARD FALK

It is good to be still alive. I enjoy this wonderful world, and the sheer excitement of life, far too much to depart before my time. I have never felt particularly close to death before and even now many months after my heart attack I find it difficult to believe it really happened.

But it did and I am damaged, physically just a little and psychologically quite a lot. That I caused my own heart attack there is very little doubt. The evidence screamed at me for years and I always took the traditional view that must have killed so many people—I can ignore the risks to my health because it will never happen to me.

I cannot change myself or my personality. I am an extrovert, a bouncing and rather aggressive individual but thankfully I also have a sense of humour and you certainly need that if you want to recover from serious illness. Laughter, even inside a cardiac ward of a hospital or in intensive care, is a superlative therapy.

If you add up the reasons why I had a heart attack then the list stretches from here to eternity.

But in fairness to my own commonsense I have stopped smoking. The craving is there and I cadge the occasional drag from those still at it. I attend a class three times a week at the City Gym in London where I am learning relaxation exercises to relieve a lot of the tension and stress in my body and to keep generally fit.

I also watch my diet closely. There is a higher level of cholesterol in my blood than there should be if I wish to receive the Queen's telegram when I reach a hundred. I am now careful about the amount of saturated fat in my food. It might take a little time but I am beginning to enjoy low-fat spreads instead of butter, yoghurt instead of cream and I now have red meat about two or three times a week and eat more chicken and fish instead.

For the future I am aware that the greatest challenge is to ensure that the good resolutions which followed my heart attack are continued for the rest of my life. A healthy lifestyle is pointless if you only adopt it for a few months and then creep back into the bad old ways. The safeguards I must take to protect my health are for life and those who wait for a heart attack before they change are clearly just as dumb as I was.

Of course I have to thank the old doc, Roger Blackwood, for keeping me going so far and inspiring me to write this book. If I live to old age then his care, skill and advice, coupled with a bit of effort from me, will have made it possible.

Lurking in the back of my mind is the thought that if I can keep going for a few more years then medical science will be catching up. But this is only a probability. The reality is that survival is really up to me.

There is a man I became very close to in hospital. I remember Tony, and watching him lying on his back gasping for breath, suffering from such chronic heart disease that a transplant was the only chance of prolonging his life for a few years and he did undergo a successful operation. But I thought to myself as this very brave man suffered just how can we stop so many individual tragedies on such a massive scale? Imagine four stadiums like Wembley all packed solid. That's 400,000 people, the number who become yet another statistic in Britain's killer disease.

It's why I wrote the book with Roger. We beg you to ask, 'Why kill yourself?'

And then change your life to prevent it.

ROGER BLACKWOOD

From my point of view it was very interesting writing this book. Only by sitting and thinking about the numerous problems which surround a heart attack have I been able to clarify in my own mind how I should approach patients in this situation. It's all too easy as a doctor to concentrate on the physical side of a patient's condition and to ignore the psychological aspects.

Smoking is dangerous. It damages the
heart. You must stop.

Only by talking to Bernard in great depth have I realised how little we actually do as doctors in coping with the patient as a whole. A direct result of this association with Bernard is the setting up of a formal rehabilitation programme for my own hospital and district. This involves space, people and money. Hopefully some of the profits from this book will go directly to that venture.

From Bernard's point of view I think writing this book was much more of a strain than he is prepared to admit. He has had to relive his heart attack over and over again at a time when he should be forgetting about it altogether. It has been his energy and a genuine desire to help others that have resulted in the book being produced so quickly, and I admire the way he has tried to resume his normal active life coupled with a positive attitude to changing his lifestyle. Bernard is a 'survivor' and this demonstrates that if the will is there you can overcome any problem that appears.

Writing this book can only confirm the importance of preventive medicine. However tempting it is to be exploring the frontiers of technology it must never be to the exclusion of trying to prevent heart disease before it occurs. This is also a responsibility of government which should provide funds for a national effort, perhaps on the same campaigning lines we have successfully started in Slough.

All the concern about diseases like AIDS is very laudable because if we are aware of the disease process before it reaches epidemic proportions then something can be done to save many lives. Heart attacks have become so much a way of life in this country that we just accept them as inevitable. With the benefit of hindsight it is a pity we did not have an adequate preventive campaign in the 1960s.

But it is never too late to start.

Appendix: The Slough Health Habit

DR ROGER BLACKWOOD

As a Senior Registrar at the John Radcliffe in Oxford I spent
most of my time finding beds for patients rather than practising
medicine. It seemed to be such a waste of time after all the
years of training. Now, as a consultant, my junior staff rightly
complain that they spend far too much time finding beds. It
is a permanent hassle. Any scheme that prevents people from
becoming ill in the first place would seem to make a lot of
sense. And rather than leaving it to other people, a consultant
should take an active part in promoting it.

This was the background to the *Slough Health Habit*, a
pioneering scheme designed to involve the entire community
of Slough with its population of 100,000 people.

The campaign is to reduce the incidence of heart disease in
this one town by making everyone more aware of the primary
risk factors, and how they can begin to eliminate them both
as individuals and as a community. It is hoped that it will set
a pattern for a national effort.

Along with the community physician of the district, we
decided that the programme should take place using the frame-
work of existing employees of the District Health Authority
except for specialised jobs where we had no expertise, such as
computing. Our initial budget was nil. Soon after its initiation,
the community physicians put their weight behind the scheme
and the Health Promotion group, also part of the District
Health Authority, took on the task of educating Slough.

What surprised me was the enormous enthusiasm displayed
by everyone. Once the District Health Authority had formally
approved the programme we went to talk to the Slough Town
Council. Again we had a superb reception and ever since have
had the utmost cooperation from them in every way.

Successive mayors have come to every Slough Health Habit

function to which they have been asked. The town's Education group have allowed us free access to the schools. Once we were underway, the Health Education Council gave us a grant of £10,000. The Family Practitioner Council allowed us to monitor new cases of heart attacks occurring in the various practices, and over the last eighteen months we have had substantial grants from both the Oxford Regional Health Authority as well as our own District Health Authority. We cannot have too high a praise for all those bodies. We have had no hassle whatever from the 'political' side and the money has allowed us to get on with the project.

Our first major venture was a video about the whole programme to be shown to schools, clubs, hospitals and at any lecture or gathering we could think of. With a further very generous grant of £10,000 from a private company and almost free services from another we filmed the video in and around Slough. Terry Wogan, Ernie Wise, Frank Bough and Dr Miriam Stoppard all contributed personally to the video free of charge. Such kindness was greatly appreciated. The result was a video that everyone would take notice of. It explained the general programme and that was followed by three monthly periods of attacking one risk factor at a time.

We started with exercise, appropriately in the spring, for exercise is always associated with that time of year (it's difficult to think of your heart and health when eating Christmas dinner). After exercise followed diet, smoking, blood pressure and stress. After this the cycle will repeat itself.

Just before we got underway the Senior Registrar in Community Medicine launched the first questionnaire into people's attitudes to heart disease. About 600 people answered.

Most thought that obesity and stress were the main risk factors for heart disease, although between 60 and 70 per cent did know of most of the other problems associated with heart disease, i.e. smoking, diet and blood pressure. When it came to detail risk factors, there was a lot of confusion. A good many thought that margarine caused heart attacks! Many knew that fat was bad for you but never cut it off their meat. Most of the smokers had tried to give up smoking but failed. Very few people had gone to their doctor specifically to have their blood pressure checked. One surprise was that over 80 per cent of the group had had their blood pressure checked in the last five years when they visited their GP with some other complaint. So perhaps primary care is working well. Another interesting finding was that brown bread was consumed by a much higher proportion of social class 1 than social class 5 and that there was a gradual increase of awareness through all the social classes up to social class 1. Having obtained this basic data we are repeating a similar questionnaire now, to see if we have influenced the population.

As far as highlighting the programme goes: We started in early spring with a Fun-Run through Slough ending at a large Health Fair in one of the local parks. We then distributed an information pack about the Slough Health Habit to all 30,000 households in Slough. During the spring and summer there was a cycle ride through Slough, a keep-fit and dance event, a swimming gala and a competition in the schools for designing a sports complex, resulting in the winning school receiving £200 worth of gymnastic equipment and the winning children receiving bicycles.

We then began to produce healthy menus and distribute them in Slough as well as formal talks with the School Catering Service. At a presentation to industry in Slough we not only presented the project but also gave those attending a healthy lunch. Another health meal was prepared for a large group at Slough Technical College at the end of a training course for NHS employees and technical college staff in healthy catering. A local dairy distributed free of charge diet information packs to many households in Slough. On another occasion they distributed samples of a new health breakfast cereal which had been given to us.

Then came the smoking campaign with a specially organised free pack on how to give up smoking. We had a sponsored no-smoking day when a group went round the main shopping area trying to encourage everyone to throw away their cigarettes into a huge specially designed cigarette which was towed around on a float. We have purchased two carbon monoxide monitors which test the amount of carbon monoxide in the lungs of smokers. It is also a good test of whether they have given up smoking.

Next came blood pressure. We have managed to take the

blood pressure of every child at school in Slough and on several occasions have got up blood-pressure-taking facilities in Slough High Street and in a number of local factories. Some people have eventually ended up at my outpatients clinic.

We are distributing a stress pack which includes, free of charge, a tape to enable you actively to fight against the problem.

Over the last year we have been running Fitness Testing Clinics. People walk in from the street and are measured for height and weight, tested for blood pressure, measured for the amount of fat (by using calipers) and given a simple submaximal exercise test on a bicycle. At the end of the test their fitness is graded and surprisingly less than 5 per cent come out above average. Such is its popularity that although we have done well over 2,000 tests we have an eight-week waiting list for the 'booked' sessions.

We have widely distributed car stickers, badges and pens and we have had frequent articles—almost weekly—in the local press. I have also lectured in school assemblies on numerous occasions.

So this is what the programme is and it is still creating great enthusiasm. It was certainly worth starting the Slough Health Habit although its benefit will not be seen for many years to come. It is the Health Prevention Unit which deserves the credit for the success of the campaign as a result of their considerable enthusiasm and professionalism.